Pilot's Wings of the United States

Civilian and Commercial

1913 - 1995

by

Philip R. Martin

with color photography and cover design by Tracy Conn

1996

ISBN   0-930968-01-8

Beach Cities Publishing Co.

Long Beach, California, U.S.A.   90809-1051

Published by Beach Cities Publishing Co.
P.O. Box 91051, 3640 E. Tenth Street,
Long Beach, CA USA 90809-1051
310-434-6701

© Philip R. Martin, 1996

All rights reserved. All material contained may not be reproduced by any means, including electronic, without prior written permission from the publisher. Civil and criminal legal remedies apply.

We recognize that some logo entries herein contained are the property of the trademark holder. We use them for identification purposes only.

The information contained in this book is provided for informational purposes. It contains our best evaluation of data provided at the time of printing. It should not in any way be relied upon as a source of authenticity of any picture, image or description in this book. We are not responsible for any errors, omissions or mis-statements.

Library of Congress Catalog Card Number 93-90426

Library of Congress Cataloging-in-Publication Data
Martin, Philip R.
    Pilot's Wings of the United States
    Civilian and Commercial Wings -1913-1995
  / Philip R. Martin

ISBN 0-930968-01-8

Printed and bound in the United States of America

ACKNOWLEDGMENTS

I WOULD VERY MUCH LIKE TO THANK THE FOLLOWING INDIVIDUALS, ORGANIZATIONS AND COMPANIES FOR UN-SELFISHLY CONTRIBUTING ASSISTANCE, INFORMATION AND / OR WINGS TO PHOTOGRAPH FOR THIS BOOK.
THANK YOU VERY MUCH FOR YOUR HELP !

Dianne Abbott, California Wing Specialties
Ace Avakian, Frontier Airlines
Aircraft Owners and Pilots Association (AOPA)
Airline Pilots Association (ALPA)
Patricia Bonner
Keith Boyer, San Diego Aerospace Museum
Dilsie L. Brown, Midway Airlines
Len Burke, Captain, Air Cal-American Airlines
Ron Burkey
Dave Cherkis
Paul Collins, World Airline Hist. Soc. (WAHS)
Command Airways, Inc.
Tracy Conn
O. Gregory DeMille, O.C. Tanner Co.
Frank Fato, Chief Pilot, Federal Express
Daniel Fox, American Eagle / Flagship Airlines
Barbara Freeman, Southwest Airlines
Marti Furman, MacDonnell-Douglas Aircraft
Bill and Sue Gawchick, Pan American
Lionel D. Ginsburg.
Jim Gordon
John Hazlet, Ameriflight, Inc
Kylee Hickok, Era Aviation
Grace S. Hilton, PCA and EAL Capt.'s wife
Dave Hulan, Director Flt.Ops., Airlift International
John Joiner, Delta Airlines
Randy Jones, Tarpy Tailors, LAX
Don Kerr, Captain, Trump Exp & USAir Shuttle
Deborah L. Ketner, Suburban Airlines
R.L. Koran, Captain, American Airlines
L.A. Bennett, LAB Flying Services, Alaska

Ralph C. Lewis, Transocean A/L & United A/L
Edwin McKellar, Dir., San Diego Aerospace Museum
Russell McKnire, Rocky Mountain Express
Dennis C. Mosseller, Chief Pilot, Southwest Airlines
Edie Nelson, Transocean Airlines
Vicki Newcomer
Lyman Nichols, 630 North & Royal Hawaiian A/L
Pam Ott
Caitlin Ott-Conn
Travis Ott-Conn
Tom Peters, Chief Pilot, Carnival Airlines
Marshall Pumphrey, Trans World Airlines
Floyd Ririe, Captain, Frontier Airlines
John Russell, Pan American Airlines
D.C. Sanderlin, American International Airways
Bruce Shuey, California Wing Specialties
Ernie Siracusa
Hank Smith, LGB, Insights
Clark Skillman, American Eagle & McClain
Hank Smith, TOA
Bill Stritzel, Silver Flight
Sarah P. Sproul, Mesa Airlines, Inc.
Penn R. Stohr, Evergreen International Airlines
Dian K. Sutherland, DHL WorldwidE
Arue Szura, Transocean Airlines
Merle Thomas
Marshall Tilley, ValuJet Airlines
Peter Walton, Heraldry of the Air Museum
Cooper Weeks, TWA, Captain
Robert A. Westhoff, United Express
Robert L. Weir, Zantop International Airlines

**Over the six years which it took to complete this book, it is quite possible to forget some one or some company for its help.
To those unspoken contributors - Thank you, also !**

PREFACE

You've seen them walking through airport terminals and at air shows, those pilots with their wings showing proudly on their uniforms and jackets. What does all that symbolism mean? Well, besides a sign of achievement, those wings attest to their employment and are also a corporate symbol of trust and responsibility. It represents a sizable trust in the individual. He or she has met certain standards to be in charge of and responsible for people, like you and me, and cargo which maybe worth large amounts of money. This is not to mention the million dollars invested in the aircraft they fly. They must always be able to perform at the highest level, and sometimes in the most adverse weather and conditions. We are generally in awe of these individuals who challenge the skies. I think immediately about aviation heroes such as Charles Lindbergh, Amelia Erhardt and Chuck Yeager, among many, many others.

I was fortunate to be able to meet and talk with Captain Al Haynes, the skipper of the UAL DC-10 that cart wheeled on landing in Sioux City, Iowa after a complete hydraulic failure. United Airlines' faith in him was upheld by his first class performance under extreme duress. You could say , "He more than earned his wings." Personally, I don't know of any pilots who are not proud of their wings and feel a certain satisfaction about having earned them.

During my graduate school days, the professors would be quick to point out that bachelor and master degrees were awarded or conferred on students, while doctorates were earned. A pilot's wings are the Ph.D. diplomas of aviation.

The companies included in the following pages are historically important. They were, and still are, the risk-takers in new and uncertain businesses - airlines and air travel. There are many other books which explain the stories, power struggles and plots which created and destroyed aviation empires since the 1920's. Those details I will leave to others who tell it better than I could.

I must include the following excerpt from a handout given to Pan American passengers during the Boeing Stratocrusier days of the late 1940's. It is entitled <u>Meet Your Clipper Captain</u>. It was sent to me by Barbara Freeman of Texas. It expresses, in the words of those days, the admiration felt about these "earned" symbols and the people who wear them.

... *dedicated to your service*

Pan American flight insignia stand for skill, service and integrity the world over ... and proud men wear them. Men who have successfully mastered the skills necessary to achieve outstanding success in their chosen professions.

One such insignia is worn by the men who serve you at the controls of every Pan American Flying Clipper ... the Wings of your Clipper Captain.

He belongs to a group of seasoned and highly trained flying Captains. Men whose names are linked with some of the greatest achievements in civilian and military aviation history. Men who proudly combine their personal reputations and flying experience in the one World's Most Experienced Airline ... Pan American World Airways.

Over 3,655,000 hours ... 584,804,000 miles ... more than 2640 trips to the moon.

That's Pan American's flight record symbolized by the "PAA Wings" so coveted by the Clipper Captain in charge of your flight; so respected by the tens of thousands of ground crewmen working all over the globe to make Clipper service the finest service.

But we'd like you to know more about these Master Craftsmen of Air Travel. Come with us for a moment into the Control Cabin and meet a typical Clipper Captain. Learn what his wings represent ... what he has to do to win them.

Typically he averages 20 years experience during which he has flown more than 25 different types of aircraft. He has flown to all six continents ... made scores of transocean crossings.

Before joining Pan American he was a more than competent pilot. For him to qualify as a Clipper Captain, however, Pan American added 5 years additional post graduate study.

And once he wins his Clipper wings, he must continue to prove his ability. He must pass rigid physical examinations every six months and, together with his crew , is brought in at regular intervals for "team training" in all new and advanced operating procedures as they are developed and proven.

Assisting the Captain are his first and second officer, both of whom are well qualified as command pilots. The first officer is responsible for your Clipper's proper loading - the second officer is the Magellan of the Skies, your navigator. The fourth man in the Control Cabin is the flight engineer. His control panel of over 40 instruments tells him the Clipper's exact mechanical performance, both on ground and during flight.

Finally, and so important to your personal comfort, you have your cabin flight attendants and it would take volumes to tell of the many personalized services they stand ready to provide. So, because actions speak louder than words, here is one chapter in Pan American's Service history you can write for yourself. The facts will unfold before your eyes from the moment you step aboard your Flying Clipper.

This is your Clipper Captain and crew. Their reputations and experience soar to new heights with every Clipper take-off.

• • • • • • •

INTRODUCTION

If I had known six years ago, what it would take to do this book, I **never** would have done it. This started out as a desire to, some how, organize my collection of U.S. Commercial wings. I had no idea how many airlines and other commercial air interests there were who fly or have fleets. As you will see there are 456 listings, with over 700 images contained in this book.

Anytime a person sits down to do something which has never been done before, it is necessary to face the reality that there will be the inevitable mistakes, omissions and oversights. Hopefully, there will be only a very few of these faults found in these listings. If you, as my reader, understand that this is the first work dealing with U.S. Commercial Pilot Wings, I would hope that you will give me some space to correct mistakes in subsequent editions.

While trying to extract the truth and establish the facts surrounding these listings, I needed to keep in mind that there are some "sea stories" out there about the "good old days" when flying was done by following light beacons on the ground, and engines were started by "hand-propping." It is somehow human nature to remember past days as somehow faster, quicker, larger and more dangerous, most of the time, then they actually were. There were plenty of situations, however, just as dangerous and more so than remembered. Of course, landing in pastures until the weather got better was not an unusual occurrence in the early days of commercial aviation. Indeed "hangar flying" and stories have their place, but my goal here is to be as accurate with the facts as I can and simply report them.

In this book I will try to show some of the heraldry of aviation. These are the images which represent the achievement, courage, precision and skill by aviators and worn with a justified pride of accomplishment their wings !

Requests from Me

I would hope that if you have good information, which would serve the airline and aviation enthusiast and other readers of this book, you would send it along and allow it to be included for everyone in the next edition. I am always interested in improving and increasing the base of knowledge.

I am ever the collector. If you have wings or other airline or aviation items which you wish to dispose of, either to sell or trade, please contact me. If I don't have a home for it, I know others who would be excited about receiving the items.

If you have a PC or Mac and use the Internet, please visit my home page at :

http://home.fia.net/~wingman/

PLEASE, READ ME NOW !!!

There is a certain ownership to all this work under U.S. Federal and International copyright laws and this is, once more, notification to you of those laws. They are very specific as to unauthorized duplication and distribution of copyrighted materials. As you will notice each listing page of this book has my copyright notice, I mean it.

No copies of any kind are permitted without prior <u>written</u> permission.

FREE TO ALL !!!

The use of the **"Airline Codes"** as provided in Appendix 1, is made available **free to all** with no restrictions.

WINGS

If you don't have much experience with wings, this might be the place to discuss wings in general as well the methodology used in this book. There are certain aspects of wings which are common to most. These have to do with types of manufacture, materials used to make the wing, hallmarks, fasteners and reproductions, restrikes .

Method of Manufacture

To properly see the following descriptions one should have, at minimum, a 10X jeweler's eye loop or magnifying glass.

There are basically two ways wings are manufactured or made. Either they are **die-struck or cast** .

Die-struck or "struck" wings are made with a large machine press which impacts a piece of metal with very high pressure in such a way as to produce an image likeness of the die. It's like a cookie-cutter in operation on dough. The die punches out a wing and leaves an image on the surface. On the edges of the wings this leaves a set of short parallel lines or "die-marks". These will run from the front of the wing to the back along the edges. You can call them lines, marks or striations if you like. Our U.S. coins are made using the die-strike method and there are these die-marks on our coin change. Virtually all professional wing manufacturers use the die-struck process.

A **cast** wing is just that - cast. A hardened mold is made of the wing image and this hallowed-out mold is then filled with a heated liquid metal. Anything from pot metal to gold can be used.

Characteristically, a cast wing has a margin or border along the thin edges where the two mold halves meet. There also can be areas of excess thin metal at the seams. The surface material may be "pock-marked" or have small holes on the surface, showing a molten metal "bubble" existed at one time. Some caution must be stated about well worn die-struck wings because they can sometimes be mistaken for a cast wing.

The overall size of the cast wing can be from 5% to 6% smaller than the original. Some jewelry is made like this, but wings with only some very early exceptions, are struck and not cast. I would look at a rare wing to see if it was cast, indicating it might be a reproduction (see definition ahead).

The Back of the Wing

The back of the wing will sometimes have **hallmarks**. The **hallmark** may tell us what type of metal was used to make the wing, usually gold or silver and content. Manufacturers may also use hallmarks as their means of identification.

We can also note the type of fastener used:

Clutch-Backs (CB), Pin-Backs (PB), or **Screwbacks (SB)**

<u>**Clutch-Backs (CB)**</u> use two sharpened posts on each side of the wing with a cap or holder for securing it to cloth.
<u>**Pin-Backs (PB)**</u> are straight pins placed on a hinge on one side of the wing extending to a clasp on the other side.
<u>**Screwbacks (SB)**</u> are posts on each side of the wing which are threaded to accept a metal to cloth nut.

There doesn't seem to be any age connection on these fasteners. PB's and SB's have been used since the earliest wings through todays wings. CB's were used as early as the mid to late1930's through today.

Materials Used

Most modern wings are made from non-precious or in-expensive common metals. The use of precious metals for wings is found less and less often, primarily due to the increased cost. Consequently, more sterling silver, gold, and gold-filled wings will be found prior to the late 1950's and 1960's than today. In some cases there will be a combination of metals used in the wings.

For the purposes of this book, I have used the following descriptions which convey the color and material of the metal and bullion (see next page) wings:

<u>**Bronzetone**</u> - the use of a bronze coloring, coating or paint so as to appear like bronze

<u>**Bronze**</u> - the use of copper and zinc, usually mixed 70% to 30%, under the heat of fusion to produce a bronze wing

<u>**Goldtone**</u> - the use of a gold coloring, coating or paint so as to appear like gold

Gold-Filled - application of gold particles to the wing of at least 5% or 10%. Gold-filled hallmarks usually indicate the fractional content of the gold, e.g., 1/10 or 1/20 GF

Gold-Plated - uses electricity to apply gold particles to the wing while emersed in a special solution

Rolled Gold - a lamination of a thin sheet of gold over a different type of metal, usually brass or bronze, applied under heat to give a durable gold outer layer

Gold - solid gold and hallmarked as to the quality of the gold, e.g., 10kt, 14kt or 18kt

> The content of gold in **10 kt.** is about **41.7%**.
> The content of gold in **14 kt.** is about **57.5%**.
> The content of gold in **18 kt.** is about **75%**.

Greentone - use of a material which gives a decided "green" tone or patina to the surface of the wing

Greytone - use of a material which gives a decided "grey" tone or patina to the surface of the wing

Silvertone - the use of a silver coloring, coating or paint so as to appear like silver

Silver - Filled - requires at least 1/20th silver content

Coin Silver - uses of at least 90% pure silver in the wing

Sterling - uses of at least 92.5% pure silver in the wing

Bullion Wings

The **bullion** wing is another type of wing made of cloth, generally black or brown cotton or wool. The wing itself is designed by using metallic or colored thread patterns sewn directly onto the cloth. The metallic thread, called "bullion" gives this wing its name. The centers can be a solid metal disc or shape with the company's logo on it.

Reproductions and Restrikes

A **Reproduction** is a copy. It is not in any way an original. Reproductions are usually cast and when viewed with a 10X magnifying glass, show many surface holes and imperfections. Without judging intentions, the buyer of a reproduction is usually not told that it is a reproduction.

A **Restrike** is a wing which has been duplicated or remade, usually by the original maker, at a time _after_ its original production. Original dies are reused, generally by using more modern materials to duplicate the original wing. Sometimes this is done to fill requests from collectors. A restrike should never knowingly be presented as an original. There is also a separate market in restrikes.

Methodology

Entries:

Each listing includes : the company name, dates of operation, geographical area served, type of operation conducted, facts about creation, including mergers, buyouts, bankruptcies and going out of business. Where dates are not certain or histories clouded, there will be mention to those facts. You might see a phrase like - No information or 19xx - 19xx.

As far as dates of operation, there may be a year or so difference between when some say a company started and what you see here. This may be due to the company's forming in one year and actually beginning operations in the next, or terminating operations in one year, and finalizing liquidation in the next. I have tried to list only the years of operation.

The companies and agencies listed in this book are by no means a complete listing of all aviation companies, but the list includes what I have discovered to be significant for the subject of this book. Undoubtedly there were other companies who flew without pilot's wings and they are not listed here.

While a company may have had scheduled flights in a certain part of the country, they could have also been involved in international charters. I have tried to include the primary or main areas of service

There may be some discrepancies as to the final disposition of a company due to a combination of actions at its end, e.g. bankruptcy and a subsequent buyout of aircraft and/ or routes and/ or gates at certain airport locations. Nevertheless, I have tried to be as accurate as possible within the scope of these listings.

Descriptions:

In this book wings will be described to include their size, the material it is made from , the color, the texture, codes and symbols, and the use of logos.

I have assumed that each listing in this book uses pilot wings.Some may not have used any and I will indicate that when known.

I will include the illustrations/pictures of the wings when available, otherwise you will see **NATP/M** - (Not Able To Photograph or Measure). This means I assume that wings exist, but I have not seen, measured or photographed them to be cataloged.

When there are photos, these are examples of wings available to me and are not necessarily all the wings used by that company. The quality of the images will vary, since in somecases the only images available were Xerox copies.

To describe and catalog wings properly, we must consider the following in each description : the Size and Material used, and the Color and Texture.

Size & Material:

Each wing will be described by size, measured to the nearest millimeter (**MM**) at its longest horizontal point, tip to tip, using a common set of vernier calipers, and by materials used. When the wing is made of cloth, the color of the background is given with a notation of the color thread used and the center device. In the metal wing descriptions, metal color and texture will also be noted.

Color:

The issue of color has been boiled down to five general categories of color : bronze, gold, green, grey, and silver.

If the wing is not made of a precious metal, such as gold, gold filled or gold plated, or sterling silver, it will be described as "bronzetone", "goldtone", "greentone", "greytone", or "silvertone".

Texture:

I have given a surface qualifier to the color of the metal wings, i.e., flat, satin or brite. It is based on the reflectivity to light of the surface.

Flat has little or no reflective properties.
Satin has a soft finish.
Bright (or Brite) is very shiny surface

These are listed in quantitative order. If the Bright area covers more area of the wing or hat badge, it will be listed first.

Codes:

Each listing includes a three-letter code which identifies each company. Most of these codes are consistent with the International Codes used in the industry. The earlier entries are assigned codes which conform as closely as possible to their names or initials. Each wing entry is then identified by that assigned 3 letter code. The code for these entries will also appear alphabetically on a list in **Appendix 1 : Airline Codes** .

Here is an example of how the system works :

AMERICAN AIRLINES is assigned an **AAL** code.

AAL

After the 3 letter code, the next digit identifies the wing position within a sequence or series in the life of the airline or company. **1 (one)** means the first series, and so on.

If an earlier wing or hat badge is omitted and later found, it will be assigned a 0 (zero) in this sequence. So, so far we have ....

AAL-1

The second number is to categorize its overall shape. Is the wing plain or does it have a star or even a star surrounded by a wreath above the center ?

For the this digit, if it is **plain** wing, it is given a **0 (zero)**. A **star above** the center of the wing earns a **2 (two)**. While a full blown **star and wreath** gets a **5 (five)**.

So for the plain, first issue American (FO) or co-pilot, we have ....

AAL-10

B or **W** is then added at the end to denote either a **hat Badge** or a **Wing**.

AAL-10W

There are some odd situations where a specific wing is used for a different crewmember in special or specific situations, e.g. a career **Flight Engineer (FE)** and it will have a **3 (three)** or **4 (four)** designation. The **1 (one)** designation is for **Flight Attendants (FA)**.

The **AAL-10W** is the first metal wing used by **AMERICAN AIRLINES** in their early years. This particular wing was worn by a Co-Pilot or **First Officer**. We abbreviate that today and call them **FO's**. They are found in the right or co-pilots seat.

Star, Star & Wreath

The next wing in this American Airlines series, **AAL-12W** is the **Captain's** wings. It is identical to the FO's except for a star above the center logo. The **AAL-15W** is a **Check Airman** or the **Supervisory / Chief Pilot** and has a surrounding wreath outside the star.

Airlines differ quite a bit on the use of the star and the star & wreath symbols. Some companies use star and wreathes to denoted rank or seniority with additions to the basic wing, while others use a plain 10 wing for all flight deck personnel. If you see only a 15W number, there may also be a 12W and/or even a 10W to go with it. Any combination is possible.

Some early airlines had only the plain wing - 10W . Some others have just the star on all their wings - 12W . Still others have only a 15W number listed - 15W . Again, any combination is possible.

A variation on the command order may find the plain wing belonging to the **Second Officer**, or **SO**, while the FO gets the star and the Captain has both. Where this is known, I will describe it under the photograph.

Not all airlines use this star and star & wreath system. Some don't use it at all. As an example, Alaska Airlines uses their wing for all flight deck personnel. All pilots wear the same wing. There is a current rumor that they may soon add a Check Airman - a 15W.

Uniform jackets may also tell you who the Captain is by four gold stripes, and the FO has three, and the SO has two. By the way, second officers are sometime referred to as an **FE - Flight Engineer.**

Logos

When available, I have placed an example of the companies' logos or advertising, so if you have another wing or hat badge with a similar designs, you may be able to identify it. The logos are placed in a rough order as to when they were used. The copyrights of each logo rests with the respective companies and is used here only for informational and reference purposes.

Air California's first wing (ACL-10W) was a simple, but effective wing combination. The center is a metal pin of the Aztec sun calendar while the cloth wing is in the airline's uniform colors. This wing was issued to Len Burke, one of the first Air California pilots and now with American Airlines.

The earliest U.S. Air Mail wing (USM - 10W) is 14kt. gold and has a center screwlug in addition to the regular 2 screw back fasteners. These are hallmarked as to the gold content and were used by Delta, Northwest and United during the 1928-39 period. Northwest Airlines continues to use this design with a slight difference. The equator does not bisect the word "Air."

A Braniff Airways (BRN -10W) shows the 1930's depiction of the early days of commercial airline travel. Pictured is a stylized early Boeing above the sunny Southwest and South America with its palm trees. This early example did not survive without loosing some of its paint.

An early and rare Delta Airlines (DAL - 20W) silver bullion wing. Using silver metallic thread and a blue cloth center, few examples have survived. It was the forerunner of the later famous Delta "widgit" - its three color, immediately recognizable logo.

© PHILIP R. MARTIN 1995 ALL RIGHTS RESERVED. NO REPRODUCTION IN ANY FORM.

The first issue Flying Tiger Airline hat badge and wing (FTL - 10B & FTL - 10W) capitalized on their famous World War II trademark - the shark's teeth painted on their P-40's in China. These are sterling and hallmarked LGB.

I have included Frontier Airline's (FAL - 10W) with it's unique indian logo in this group. This one was issued to one of their first and most experienced pilots, Floyd Rire.

Here is a Frontier Airline's presentation wings from the FAL - 20W series. Unlike the company issue wing, it has a top runner with an emerald and the airline name on each side.

This example of Mid-Continent Airline's Check Captain (MID - 15W) has a beautifully enameled three color center. The wing is made from thin sterling and screwbacked.

© PHILIP R. MARTIN 1995 ALL RIGHTS RESERVED. NO REPRODUCTION IN ANY FORM.

Pan-Am's type 2 Junior Captain group includes the hat badge, collar device and 10kt. gold wing (PAA - 22W). These are from 1930 - 44 the early Clipper era when its founder, Juan Trippe started developing South American, Trans-Atlantic and Trans-Pacific airfields, routes and systems.

This is a Pan-Am type 3 Senior Captain (PAA - 35W) ensemble including hat badge, collar device and 10kt. gold wing. By the 1945 - 59 period, Pan Am had come out of World War 2 larger and stronger and into the jet age as America's flag carrier.

It is interesting that the indian head logo followed Western Airlines out of Trans-Continental & Western Air. This Western pilot (WAL - 10W) is gold filled.

© PHILIP R. MARTIN 1995 ALL RIGHTS RESERVED. NO REPRODUCTION IN ANY FORM.

A very striking TransContinental & Western Air hat badge (TCW - 10W) uses the chief's head as the airline logo. This gold plated piece has a large screw back. The name changed in 1950 to Trans World Airlines.

King Kamehameha graces the goldtone wing of Trans Pacific Airlines pilot (TPA - 10W) and the three - colored enamel hat badge (TPA - 10B). The hat badge shows the connection to Aloha Airlines and its eventual change into Aloha in 1959.

This Bonanza hat badge and check captain's wing (BNZ - 10B & BNZ - 10W) was used in the early 1950's and it shows the signature logo and the stylized "bird" with up-sloped wings.
© PHILIP R. MARTIN 1995 ALL RIGHTS RESERVED. NO REPRODUCTION IN ANY FORM.

A

AAA AIRLINES - AAA
1977 - 1987
MIDWEST US REGIONAL CHARTER
• OUT OF BUSINESS IN 1987

S.D.A.M. (San Diego Aerospace Museum)

AAA-10W
87MM • BRONZETONE

AAXICO AIRLINES - AAX
(AMERICAN AIR EXPORT & IMPORT COMPANY)
1956 – 1965
NEW YORK TO ATLANTA
• MERGED WITH SATURN AIRWAYS IN 1965

Koran

AAX-10B　　　　　**AAX-10W**
NATM　　　　NATM • STERLING WITH A BLACK
　　　　　　　　　　ENAMEL CENTER

© PHILIP R. MARTIN 1995 ALL RIGHTS RESERVED. NO REPRODUCTION IN ANY FORM.

ABC AIRLINES - ABC
1965 - 1966
CALIFORNIA REGIONAL CARRIER
• CEASED OPERATIONS IN 1966

NATM/P

ACADEMY AIRLINES - ACD
1965 - PRESENT
SOUTHERN US CHARTER

NATM/P

AERO AMERICA - AEM
1972 - 1984
US WEST COAST-HAWAII
• CEASED OPERATIONS IN 1984

NATM/P

AERO COMMUTER - AEC
1967 - 1968
SOUTHERN CALIFORNIA
• MERGED INTO GOLDEN WEST AIRLINES IN 1969

NATM/P

AEROMARINE AIRWAYS - AME
1920 - 1923
EASTERN US
• OVEREXTENDED FINANCIALLY CEASING OPERATIONS IN 1923

NATM/P

© PHILIP R. MARTIN 1995 ALL RIGHTS RESERVED. NO REPRODUCTION IN ANY FORM.

AEROMECH - AMH
1971 - 1983
EASTERN US
• MERGED INTO WRIGHT AIR LINES IN 1983

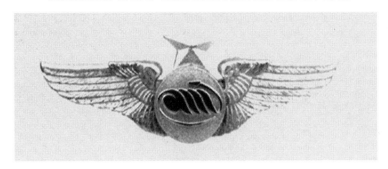

AMH-12W
79MM BRITE / SATIN GOLDTONE

AEROSTAR AIRLINES - AST
1977 - 1983
US AND CARRIBEAN

• CEASED OPERATIONS IN 1983

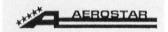

Koran

AST-1OW
NATM • BRITE SILVERTONE WITH RED & BLUE LETTER & STARS

AST-2OW
76MM BRITE/SILVERTONE
WITH BLACK WINGS

AST-25W
76MM BRITE/SILVERTONE
WITH BLACK WINGS

© PHILIP R. MARTIN 1995 ALL RIGHTS RESERVED. NO REPRODUCTION IN ANY FORM.

AIR AMERICA - AAM

1965 - 1975
WORLWIDE OPERATIONS
- EVOLVED FROM A DIVISION OF CONTINENTAL AIR LINES
- US GOVERNMENT/ CIA AIRLINE
- ENDED OPERATIONS AT THE END OF THE VIETNAM WAR

AAM-10W
80MM "SILVER" MARKED

AAM-20W
53MM STERLING

AAM-22W
53MM STERLING

AAM-25W
53MM STERLING

AAM-28W
53MM SILVERTONE WITH A BLUE CENTER

© PHILIP R. MARTIN 1995 ALL RIGHTS RESERVED. NO REPRODUCTION IN ANY FORM.

AIR AMERICA - AMI
1982 - 1983
ALASKAN REGIONAL SERVICE
• BECAME AIR AMERICA FROM SOUTHEAST SKYWAYS IN 1982
• CHANGED NAME TO WINGS OF ALASKA IN 1983

NATM/P

AIR AMERICA - AMR
1984 - 1990
CHARTER OPERATIONS - PASSENGERS
BASED ON THE WEST COAST US • OUT OF BUSINESS 1990

AMR-10B
BRITE/SILVERTONE WITH MAROON CENTER

AMR-10W
63MM BRITE/SILVERTONE
WITH MAROON CENTER

AMR-15W
63MM BRITE/SILVERTONE
WITH MAROON CENTER

© PHILIP R. MARTIN 1995 ALL RIGHTS RESERVED. NO REPRODUCTION IN ANY FORM.

AIR ATLANTA - AAT
1985 - 1987
EASTERN US COMMUTER

• CEASED OPERATIONS 1987

AAT-10B
BRITE / SATIN SILVERTONE

AAT-10W
75MM BRITE / SATIN SILVERTONE

AAT-12W
75MM BRITE / SATIN SILVERTONE

AAT-15W
75MM BRITE / SATIN SILVERTONE

© PHILIP R. MARTIN 1995 ALL RIGHTS RESERVED. NO REPRODUCTION IN ANY FORM.

AIR CALIFORNIA (AIR CAL) - ACL

1965 - 1987
US PACIFIC COAST

- CHANGED NAME TO AIR CAL IN 1981
- BOUGHT BY AMERICAN AIRLINES IN 1987

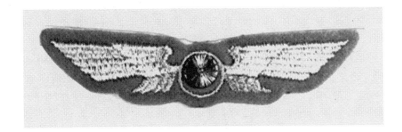

ACL-10W
86MM YELLOW CLOTH WITH GOLD BULLION & RED LOGO CENTER
AIR CALIFORNIA - 1965 - 1967

ACL-20B
SATIN GOLDTONE WITH
RED LOGO IN THE CENTER
AIR CALIFORNIA - 1968 -1975

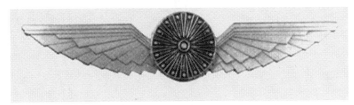

ACL-20W
86MM SATIN GOLDTONE WITH
RED LOGO IN THE CENTER
AIR CALIFORNIA - 1968 -1975

ACL-30W
90MM BRITE GOLDTONE WITH RED LOGO IN THE CENTER
AIR CALIFORNIA - 1975 -1981

© PHILIP R. MARTIN 1995 ALL RIGHTS RESERVED. NO REPRODUCTION IN ANY FORM

ACL-40B	**ACL-40W**
BRITE/ SATIN GOLDTONE	83MM BRITE/ SATIN GOLDTONE
AIR CAL 1981 - 1984	AIR CAL 1981 - 1984

ACL-50B	**ACL-50W**
FLAT GREYTONE	83MM FLAT GREYTONE
AIR CAL 1984 - 1988	AIR CAL 1984 - 1988

ACL-44W
NATM • BLACK CLOTH WITH SILVER BULLION & BROWN CENTER BACKING
AIR CAL 1981 - 1988

© PHILIP R. MARTIN 1995 ALL RIGHTS RESERVED. NO REPRODUCTION IN ANY FORM.

AIR CARGO INC. - ACU
1941 - 1944
US • QUIT(UAL,AIRLINES,EAL.TWA)

NATM/P

AIR CHAPPARAL - ACQ
1978 - 1983
ARIZONA AND CALIFORNIA
• OPERATED UNDER INLAND EMPIRE AIRLINES • BANKRUPT IN 1983

NATM/P

AIR CONTINENTAL - NAR
1979 - 19XX
MID-WEST US CHARTER
• UNKNOWN

NATM/P

AIR FLIGHT AIRLINES - AFA
19 XX - 1987
MIDWEST CHARTER
• MAY HAVE USED "INTERNATIONAL" IN NAME • OUT OF BUSINESS IN 1987

AFA-15W
62MM BRITE GOLDTONE

© PHILIP R. MARTIN 1995 ALL RIGHTS RESERVED. NO REPRODUCTION IN ANY FORM.

AIR FLORIDA - AFL
1971 - 1985
EASTERN US / CARRIBEAN / EUROPE
- MERGED WITH AIR SUNSHINE IN 1978
- ACQUIRED BY MIDWAY AIRLINES IN 1985

AFL-10W
83MM SATIN GOLDTONE

AFL-20B
BRITE/SATIN GOLDTONE
WITH RED "AF" ON WHITE DISC

AFL-20W
80MM BRITE/SATIN GOLDTONE
WITH RED "AF" ON WHITE DISC

AFL-22W
80MM BRITE/SATIN GOLDTONE
WITH RED "AF" ON WHITE DISC

AFL-25W
80MM BRITE/SATIN GOLDTONE WITH RED "AF" ON WHITE DISC

© PHILIP R. MARTIN 1995 ALL RIGHTS RESERVED. NO REPRODUCTION IN ANY FORM.

AFL-32W
80MM BRITE/SATIN GOLDTONE
WITH WHITE "AF" ON BLUE DISC

AFL-35W
80MM BRITE/SATIN GOLDTONE
WITH WHITE "AF" ON BLUE DISC

AIR GRAND CANYON - AGC
1972 - PRESENT
GRAND CANYON SCENIC OPERATION

AIRLINE STATES THAT PILOTS DO NOT HAVE WINGS

AIR HAWAII - AHW
1977 - 1982
HAWAIIAN COMMUTER

- PURCHASED ISLAND PACIFIC AIR IN 1977
- PURCHASED AIR MOLOKAI IN 1978
- ABSORBED OAHU & KAUAI AIRLINES (OK AIR) IN 1980
- BANKRUPT IN 1982

NATM/P

AIR HOLIDAY - AHO
19 XX -19 XX
UNKNOWN

AHO-10W
81MM SATIN / BRITE GOLDTONE W/ BLACK CENTER & LOGO

AIR ILLINOIS - AIL
1970 - 1986
CENTRAL US REGIONAL CARRIER
- MERGED INTO OCEAN AIR IN 1986

NATM/P

AIR KENTUCKY AIRLINES - AKY
1974 - 1991
REGIONAL COMMUTER
- OPERATED AS ALLEGHENY COMMUTER
  AND LATER AS A US AIR COMMUTER
- OUT OF BUSINESS IN 1991

NATM/P

AIR LA - AQR
1980 - 1990
CALIFORNIA COMMUTER

- OUT OF BUSINESS 1990

AQR-10W
75MM SATIN / BRITE GOLDTONE RED LETTERS IN WHITE CENTER

AIR LOGISTICS - ALG
1973 - 19XX
SOUTHERN US
- HELICOPTER & FIXED WING

NATM / P

AIR MICRONESIA - AMC
1967 - PRESENT
SOUTH PACIFIC AREA
- SUBSIDIARY OF CONTINENTAL AIRLINES

AMC-10W
96MM BLACK CLOTH WITH YELLOW WINGS & US FLAG IN CENTER

© PHILIP R. MARTIN 1995 ALL RIGHTS RESERVED. NO REPRODUCTION IN ANY FORM.

AMC-15W
96MM BLACK CLOTH WITH YELLOW WINGS & US FLAG IN CENTER

AIR MIDWEST - AMW
1965 - 1991
CENTRAL US CARRIER
• SOLD ASSETS TO MESA AIRLINES IN 1991

AMW-10W
68MM FLAT GOLDTONE

AIR MOLOKAI - TRO
1968 - PRESENT
HAWAIIAN ISLAND COMMUTER

NATM/P

© PHILIP R. MARTIN 1995 ALL RIGHTS RESERVED. NO REPRODUCTION IN ANY FORM.

AIR NATIONAL - ANL
1983 - 1987
CHARTER US AND EUROPE

- BANKRUPT IN 1987

ANL-10W
84MM SATIN GOLDTONE WITH LOGO ON DARK BLUE CENTER

- This airline gained notoriety after abandoning several planeloads of tourists in Europe during the summer of 1987.

AIR NEVADA - ANV
1974 - PRESENT
CALIFORNIA & NEVADA COMMUTER

- FORMED IN 1974 OUT OF CAPAIR AIR TAXI

NATM/P

AIR NEW ENGLAND - ANE
1970 - 1981
EAST COAST US
- OUT OF BUSINESS IN 1981

ANE-10W
80MM SATIN GOLDTONE WITH RED LETTERS

© PHILIP R. MARTIN 1995 ALL RIGHTS RESERVED. NO REPRODUCTION IN ANY FORM.

ANE-20W
72MM FLAT SILVERTONE MULTI-
COLOR IN RED CENTER

ANE-30W
83MM SATIN SILVERTONE LOGO
WITH BLUE CENTER

AIR NEW ORLEANS - ANF
1982 - 1990
SOUTHERN US COMMUTER

• CEASED OPERATIONS IN 1990

ANF-10W
77MM BRITE / SATIN GOLDTONE, MUSTARD CENTER & BLACK LETTERS

ANF-25W
80MM BRITE GOLDTONE WITH DARK BROWN CENTER

AIR NIAGARA - ANY
1982 - 19XX
EAST COAST US REGIONAL CARRIER
• UNKNOWN

NATM/P

© PHILIP R. MARTIN 1995 ALL RIGHTS RESERVED. NO REPRODUCTION IN ANY FORM.

AIR NORTH - ANR
1972 - 1986
NORTHEAST US COMMUTER

- 1956 - BEGAN AS NORTHERN AIRWAYS
- 1970 - NAME CHANGE TO AIR NORTH
- OPERATED AS ALLEGHENY COMMUTER IN 1979
- CHANGED NAME TO BROCKWAY AIR (VT) IN 1986
- OUT OF BUSINESS IN 1986

Koran

ANR-12W
NATM • SILVERTONE

AIR ONE - AOA
1981 - 1984
CENTRAL AND EASTERN US CHARTER

- CEASED OPERATIONS IN 1984

AOA-10W
80MM BRITE GOLDTONE WITH
HORIZONTZAL RED LINE AT LOWER CENTER

© PHILIP R. MARTIN 1995 ALL RIGHTS RESERVED. NO REPRODUCTION IN ANY FORM.

AIR PAC - APC
1975 - 19 XX
ALASKAN COMMUTER
- UNKNOWN

NATM/P

AIR RESORTS AIRLINES - ARE
1975 - PRESENT
SOUTHWEST US COMMUTER

NATM/P

AIR SOUTH - SHW
1978 - 1992
SOUTHERN US CHARTER
- OUT OF BUSINESS IN 1992

NATM/P

AIR SPUR - ASQ
1981 - 19 XX
SOUTHERN CALIFORNIA COMMUTER HELICOPTERS
- OUT OF BUSINESS

NATM/P

AIR TRANSPORT COMMAND - ATC
1941 - 1945
WORLDWIDE
- WW2 NON-COMBAT, AIR TRANSPORT SERVICE USING MAINLY COMMERCIAL PILOTS
- DISBANDED AFTER END OF WORLD WAR 2
- REMAINER EVOLVED INTO MILITARY AIR TRANSPORT SERVICE (MATS)

ATC-10W
89MM BRONZETONE

ATC-12W
89MM BRONZETONE

ATC-15W
89MM BRONZETONE

ATC WINGS WERE REPRODUCED AT DIFFERENT TIMES OVER THE YEARS. REPRODUCTIONS CAN BE IDENTIFIED BECAUSE THEY ARE ABOUT 5% SMALLER THAN THE ABOVE MEASUREMENTS. THEY ARE ALSO USUALLY CAST WINGS.

ATC-20W
80MM STERLING SILVER
A.C.F.C. LOGO IN CENTER

ATC-30W
NATM • SILVER WITH A.C.F.C.* LOGO IN CENTER - "CIVILIAN PILOT" ON LOWER BANNER

* A.C.F.C. WAS A NON-COMBATANT WW 2 SERVICE - <u>A</u>IR <u>C</u>ORPS <u>F</u>ERRY <u>C</u>OMMAND

© PHILIP R. MARTIN 1995 ALL RIGHTS RESERVED. NO REPRODUCTION IN ANY FORM.

AIR VERMONT - AVM
1981 - 19 XX
NORTHEAST US COMMUTER
• ABSORBED IN THE BROCKWAY (VT) TWA EXPRESS SYSTEM

NATM/P

AIR VIRGINIA (AV AIR) - AVB
1979 - 1988
ATLANTIC SEABOARD COMMUTER
• ABSORBED INTO AMERICAN EAGLE COMMUTER SYSTEM IN 1988

AVB-10W
68MM FLAT SILVERTONE

AVB-20W
68MM FLAT SILVERTONE

© PHILIP R. MARTIN 1995 ALL RIGHTS RESERVED. NO REPRODUCTION IN ANY FORM.

AIR WEST - AWS
1966 - 1967
PACIFIC COAST AREA
• MERGED INTO HUGHES AIR WEST IN 1967

AWS-10B
NATM • STERLING

AWS-10W
80MM STERLING

AIR WISCONSIN - AWI
1965 - PRESENT
CENTRAL US
• MERGED WITH MISSISSIPPI VALLEY AIRLINES IN 1986
• RECENTLY ACQUIRED ASPEN AIRWAYS
• OPERATES AS UNITED EXPRESS

AWI-10B
BRITE / SATIN GOLDTONE WITH BLACK
WITH CENTER, ORANGE & GREEN LETTERS

AWI-10W
79MM BRITE / SATIN GOLDTONE
BLACK CENTER, ORANGE &
GREEN LETTERS

© PHILIP R. MARTIN 1995 ALL RIGHTS RESERVED. NO REPRODUCTION IN ANY FORM.

AIRBORNE EXPRESS - ABX
1980 - PRESENT
US AIR CARGO CARRIER

ABX-10W
86MM FLAT SILVERTONE WITH
RED LETTER ON GREY CENTER

ABX-15W
86MM FLAT SILVERTONE WITH
RED LETTER ON GREY CENTER

AIRLIFT INTERNATIONAL AIRLINES - AQL
1963 - PRESENT
INTERNATIONAL AIR CARGO & CHARTER

- CHANGED NAME FROM RIDDLE AIRLINES IN 1963
- ACQUIRED SLICK AIRWAYS IN 1966
- IN CHAPTER 11 IN 1985

AQL-10B
STERLING OR SILVERTONE

AQL-10W
79MM STERLING OR SILVERTONE

© PHILIP R. MARTIN 1995 ALL RIGHTS RESERVED. NO REPRODUCTION IN ANY FORM.

ALASKA AIRLINES - ASA

1944 - PRESENT
WEST COAST US, ALASKA, MEXICO

- STARTED AS ALASKA STAR AIRLINES IN 1937
- RENAMED ALASKA AIRLINES IN 1944
- MERGED WITH CORDOVA AIRLINES IN 1967
- MERGED WITH ALASKA COASTAL AIRLINES IN 1968
- ACQUIRED JET AMERICA IN 1986

ASA-10W
82MM BRITE SILVERTONE WITH MAROON LOGO IN CENTER

ASA-20W
80MM BRITE SILVERTONE WITH OLDER BLUE & RED LOGO

Koran

ASA-30W
NATM • BLACK CLOTH
WITH GOLD, RED & BLUE THREAD

ASA-40W
82MM BRITE GOLDTONE WITH
CURRENT LOGO IN CENTER

© PHILIP R. MARTIN 1995 ALL RIGHTS RESERVED. NO REPRODUCTION IN ANY FORM.

ALASKA AIRLINES COMMUTER
19XX - PRESENT
ALAKAN REGIONAL CARRIERS CONSISTING OF:
• BERING AIR • ERA AIRLINES • LAB FLYING SERVICE • HORIZON AIR • MARKAIR
EACH CARRIER HAS ITS WINGS LISTED SEPERATELY

ALASKA COASTAL AIRLINES - ASC
1939 - 1967
ALASKA
• MERGED WITH ELLIS AIRLINES IN 1962
• MERGED INTO ALASKA AIRLINES IN 1968

ASC-20W
NATM • BLACK CLOTH WITH RED CENTER

ALASKA INTERNATIONAL AIRLINES - AIA
1947 - 19XX
ALASKA
• ORIGINALLY FORMED IN 1947 AS INTERIOR AIRWAYS
• CHANGED NAME IN 1972 • DISPOSITION UNKNOWN

AIA-10W
78MM BRITE SILVERTONE WITH A WHITE "A" ON BLUE CENTER

© PHILIP R. MARTIN 1995 ALL RIGHTS RESERVED. NO REPRODUCTION IN ANY FORM.

ALASKAN AIRWAYS - AKA
1928 - 1936
ALASKA
- EVOLVED FROM AMERICAN AIRLINES INTO PAN AMERICAN

NATM/P

ALASKA SOUTHERN AIRWAYS - ASO
1933 - 1934
ALASKA
- BOUGHT BY PAN AMERICAN IN 1934

NATM/P

ALASKA STAR AIRLINES - ASR
1944 - 1946
ALASKA
- MERGED INTO ALASKA AIRLINES IN 1946

ASR-10W
82MM BRITE SILVERTONE WITH LIGHT BLUE CENTER

ALFRED FRANK AIRWAYS - AFR
1934 - 1941
US
- EVOLVED INTO NATIONAL PARKS AIRWAYS IN 1935
- BOUGHT BY WESTERN AIR EXPRESS IN 1937
- ULTIMATELY BECAME WESTERN AIR LINES IN 1941

NATM/P

© PHILIP R. MARTIN 1995 ALL RIGHTS RESERVED. NO REPRODUCTION IN ANY FORM.

ALLEGHENY AIRLINES - ALE
1953 - 1979
NORTHEAST US
• EVOLVED FROM ALL AMERICAN AIRLINES IN 1937
• CHANGED NAME TO ALLEGHENY IN 1953
• ACQUIRED LAKE CENTRAL AIRLINES IN 1968
• RENAMED US AIR IN 1979

ALE-20B
NATM • STERLING WITH A RED AND BLUE LOGO IN THE CENTER

ALE-20W
80MM STERLING WITH A RED AND BLUE LOGO IN THE CENTER

ALE-22W
80MM STERLING WITH A RED AND BLUE LOGO IN THE CENTER

ALE-25W
80MM STERLING WITH A RED AND BLUE LOGO IN THE CENTER

© PHILIP R. MARTIN 1995 ALL RIGHTS RESERVED. NO REPRODUCTION IN ANY FORM.

ALLEGHENY COMMUTER (US AIR COMMUTER SINCE 1979) - ALO
1968 - PRESENT
NORTHCENTRAL AND NORTHEASTERN US AIR COMMUTER
CONSISTS OF THE FOLLOWING AIRLINES :

- AIR KENTUCKY AIRLINES, IN SINCE 1974 - PRESENT
- CHATAUGUA AIRLINES, NY SINCE 1974 - PRESENT
- CROWN AIRWAYS, PA SINCE 1969 - PRESENT
- PENNSLYVANIA AIRLINES, PA SINCE 1973 - PRESENT
- POCONO AIRLINES, PA SINCE1968 - 1990
- SUBURBAN AIRLINES, PA SINCE 1973 - PRESENT

ALO-12W
80MM BRITE SILVERTONE WITH BLACK "AC" IN THE CENTER

ALLIED CHEMICAL CO. - ALI
19 XX - PRESENT
WORLWIDE
INTERNATIONAL CHEMICAL COMPANY

ALI-10W
97MM SATIN STERLING WITH LOGO & NAME IN BLUE CENTER

© PHILIP R. MARTIN 1995 ALL RIGHTS RESERVED. NO REPRODUCTION IN ANY FORM.

ALLIED SIGNAL CO. - ALS
19 XX - PRESENT
WORLWIDE
INTERNATIONAL ELECTRONICS COMPANY

ALS-10W
76MM SATIN GREENTONE

ALL AMERICAN AIRLINES - ALA
1937 - 1953
US
• MERGED INTO ALLEGEHNY AIRLINES IN 1953

ALA-22W
76MM STERLING OR FLAT SILVERTONE
WITH BLUE AIRPLANE OVER A WHITE USA IN A BROWN CIRCLE

© PHILIP R. MARTIN 1995 ALL RIGHTS RESERVED. NO REPRODUCTION IN ANY FORM.

ALL STAR AIRLINES - ALL
1983 - 1987
EAST COAST US CHARTER

- OUT OF BUSINESS IN 1987

ALL-12W
80MM SATIN SILVERTONE WITH RED & SILVER STARS ON A BLUE CENTER

ALOHA AIRLINES - AAH
1959 - PRESENT
PACIFIC REGION - WESTERN US - HAWAIIAN ISLANDS

- FOUNDED AS TRANS-PACIFIC AIRLINES 1946
- CHANGED NAME TO ALOHA AIRLINES IN 1959

AAH-10B
SATIN GOLDTONE, BLUE
FLOWER AND CIRCLE

AAH-10W
69MM SATIN GOLDTONE, BLUE
FLOWER AND CIRCLE

© PHILIP R. MARTIN 1995 ALL RIGHTS RESERVED. NO REPRODUCTION IN ANY FORM.

ALOHA ISLAND AIR - AIS
1980 - PRESENT
HAWAIIAN ISLANDS COMMUTER

AIS-10W
84MM SATIN GOLDTONE WITH BLACK CENTER

ALPHA AIR - ALH
1976 - PRESENT
WESTERN US REGIONAL COMMUTER

ALH-10W
75MM BRITE SILVERTONE
BLUE "ALPHA", RED "AIR" ON A LIGHT BLUE DIAMOND

ALTAIR AVIATION - ALT
1966 - 1982
NORTHEAST US

- FOUNDED IN PHILADELPHIA IN 1966
- OUT OF BUSINESS IN 1982

ALT-10W
82MM BRITE SILVERTONE WITH BLUE & BLACK CENTER

© PHILIP R. MARTIN 1995 ALL RIGHTS RESERVED. NO REPRODUCTION IN ANY FORM.

AMERICAN AIRLINES - AAL
1934 - PRESENT
INTERNATIONAL

- EVOLVED FROM AMERICAN AIRWAYS IN 1934
- MERGED WITH AIR CAL IN 1987

AAL-10W
83MM GOLD OR GF OVER STERLING
FIRST OFFICER
1934 - 1946

AAL-12W
83MM GOLD OR GF OVER STERLING
CAPTAIN
1934 - 1946

AAL-15W
83MM GOLD or GF OVER STERLING
CHECK CAPTAIN
1934 - 1946

AAL-17W
83MM GOLD or GF OVER STERLING
CAREER FLIGHT ENGINEER
1946 - 1959

Koran

AAL-19W
NATM • GOLD or GF OVER STERLING
CAREER FLIGHT ENGINEER
1946 - 1959

AAL-20W
83MM GOLD or GF OVER STERLING
FIRST OFFICER
1946 - 1959

- NOTE: BEFORE 1946, THE AAL EAGLE FACES TO THE LEFT AS YOU VIEW IT. AFTER 1946, THE EAGLE FACES TO THE RIGHT.

© PHILIP R. MARTIN 1995 ALL RIGHTS RESERVED. NO REPRODUCTION IN ANY FORM.

AAL-22W
83MM GOLD or GF OVER STERLING
CAPTAIN
1946 - 1959

AAL-25W
NATM • GOLD or GF OVER STERLING
CHECK CAPTAIN
1946 - 1959

AAL-30W
68MM STERLING or SF or SILVERTONE
FIRST OFFICER / FE
1960 - PRESENT

AAL-33W
68MM STERLING or SF or SILVERTONE
FIRST OFFICER / CAREER FE
1960 - PRESENT

AAL-32W
68MM STERLING OR SF or SILVERTONE
CAPTAIN
1960 - PRESENT

AAL-35W
68MM STERLING or SF or SILVERTONE
CHECK CAPTAIN
1960 - PRESENT

© PHILIP R. MARTIN 1995 ALL RIGHTS RESERVED. NO REPRODUCTION IN ANY FORM.

Koran

AAL-36W
NATM • BLACK CLOTH SILVER & BLACK THREAD

AAL-37W
68MM STERLING or SF or SILVERTONE - CAREER FLIGHT ENGINEER
1960 - PRESENT

AAL-39W
68MM STERLING or SF or SILVERTONE - CHECK FLIGHT ENGINEER
1960 - PRESENT

 # AMERICAN AIRWAYS - AMA
1930 - 1934
US
• EVOLVED INTO AMERICAN AIRLINES IN 1934

NATM/P

© PHILIP R. MARTIN 1995 ALL RIGHTS RESERVED. NO REPRODUCTION IN ANY FORM.

AMERICAN CAN COMPANY - ACO
19 XX - PRESENT
WORLD WIDE
INTERNATIONAL CAN PRODUCER

ACO-10W
75MM SATIN / BRITE GOLDTONE

AMERICAN EAGLE - AME
1984 - PRESENT
US COMMUTER AIRLINES BELONGING TO THE AMERICAN
AIRLINES COMMUTER GROUP CONSISTS OF: • AV AIR, NC SINCE 1985 - 1988
• CHAPARRAL AIRLINES, TX SINCE 1984 - PRESENT
• COMMAND AIRWAYS, NY SINCE 1986 - PRESENT
• EXECUTIVE AIR CHARTER, PR SINCE 1986
• FLAGSHIP AIRLINES, TN SINCE 19XX - PRESENT
• METRO-FLIGHT, TX SINCE 1984 - PRESENT
• NASHVILLE EAGLE, TN SINCE 1987
• SIMMONS AIRLINES, MI SINCE 1985 - PRESENT
• WINGS WEST AIRLINES, CA SINCE 1986 - PRESENT

AME-10W　　　　　　　　　　　**AME-12W**
67MM BRITE SILVERTONE　　　　67MM BRITE SILVERTONE
WITH LOWER PART BLACK　　　　WITH LOWER PART BLACK

© PHILIP R. MARTIN 1995 ALL RIGHTS RESERVED. NO REPRODUCTION IN ANY FORM.

AMERICAN EXPORT AIRLINES - AXP
1937 - 1945
INTERNATIONAL
• CHANGEDINTO AMERICAN OVERSEAS AIRLINES IN 1945

NATM/P

AMERICAN FLYERS AIRLINE CORP. - AFC
1949 - 1971
TRANSATLANTIC & MEXICO CHARTER & FREIGHT
• BOUGHT BY UNIVERSAL AIRLINES IN 1971

AFC-10W
81MM BRITE/FLAT GOLDTONE

AFC-12W
81MM BRITE/FLAT GOLDTONE

AMERICAN INTER-ISLAND - AII
1977 - 1982
AMERICAN VIRGIN ISLANDS COMMUTER
• AMERICAN AIRLINES COMMUTER REPLACED WITH REGULAR SERVICE IN 1982

AII-10W
80MM FLAT SILVERTONE

AII-12W
80MM FLAT SILVERTONE

© PHILIP R. MARTIN 1995 ALL RIGHTS RESERVED. NO REPRODUCTION IN ANY FORM.

AMERICAN INTERNATIONAL AIRWAYS - AMN
1972 - 1984
WORLDWIDE

- CARGO AND CHARTER

AMN-10W
NATM • GOLDTONE

AMERICAN INTERNATIONAL AIRLINES - AMY
1990 - PRESENT
WORLDWIDE
- CARGO AND CHARTER

AMY-10W
84MM SATIN GOLDTONE

AMERICAN OVERSEAS AIRLINES - AOV
1945 - 1950
INTERNATIONAL
- CAME FROM AMERICAN EXPORT AIRLINES IN 1945
- SOLD TO PAN AMERICAN IN 1950

NATM/P

© PHILIP R. MARTIN 1995 ALL RIGHTS RESERVED. NO REPRODUCTION IN ANY FORM.

AMERICAN TRANS AIR - AMT
1973 - PRESENT
WORLDWIDE CHARTER

• BEGAN CHARTER OPERATIONS IN 1981

AMT-10B
BLACK CLOTH, GOLD BULLION, BLACK & WHITE LOGO & SHIELD

AMT-12W
82MM SATIN GOLDTONE WITH
BLACK & WHITE LOGO & SHIELD

AMT-15W
82MM SATIN GOLDTONE WITH
BLACK & WHITE LOGO & SHIELD

AMERICA TRANS OCEANIC CO. - ATO
1919
SERVICE TO BAHAMAS
• OUT OF BUSINES IN 1919

NATM/P

© PHILIP R. MARTIN 1995 ALL RIGHTS RESERVED. NO REPRODUCTION IN ANY FORM.

AMERICA WEST AIRLINES - AWE
1983 - PRESENT
US

- ARIZONA-BASED NATIONAL CARRIER

AWE-12W
83MM FLAT SILVERTONE

AMERIJET INTERNATIONAL AIRLINES - AJT
1978 - PRESENT
US & INTERNATIONAL CHARTER

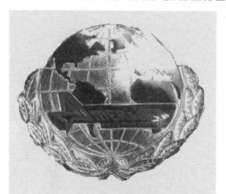

AJT-10WB
BRITE/SATIN GOLDTONE WITH LOGO

AJT-10W
83MM BRITE/SATIN GOLDTONE
LOGO ON WHITE CENTER

AJT-15W
83MM BRITE/SATIN GOLDTONE
LOGO ON WHITE CENTER

© PHILIP R. MARTIN 1995 ALL RIGHTS RESERVED. NO REPRODUCTION IN ANY FORM.

AMERIFLIGHT, INC. - AMF
1968 - PRESENT
CHARTER CARGO CARRIER

AMF-10W
65MM BRITE SILVERTONE WITH PLAIN OR RED LINED LOGO

AOPA (AIRCRAFT OWNERS & PILOT'S ASSOC.) - AOP
1957 - PRESENT
US - INTERNATIONAL

AOP -10W
74MM GOLDTONE WITH WHITE SHEILD & GOLD LETTERS ON BAND

APACHE AIRLINES - APA
1957 - 1958
SOUTHWEST US
• ACQUIRED BY FRONTIER AIRLINES IN 1958

NATM/P

© PHILIP R. MARTIN 1995 ALL RIGHTS RESERVED. NO REPRODUCTION IN ANY FORM.

ARAMCO (ARAB / AMERICAN OIL COMPANY) - ARM
19 XX - PRESENT
US - MIDDLE EAST
OIL COMPANY

ARM-10W　　　　　　　　　　　**ARM-12W**

84MM GOLD FILLED　　　　　　　84MM GOLD FILLED

ARIZONA AIRWAYS - ARZ
1945 - 1950
SOUTHWEST US
• MERGERED INTO MONARCH AIRLINES IN 1950

NATM/P

ARCO (ATLANTIC RICHFIELD OIL CO.) - ARC
1945 - 1950
SOUTHWEST US
• OIL COMPANY CORPORATE OPERATION

ARC-15W

82MM STERLING

© PHILIP R. MARTIN 1995 ALL RIGHTS RESERVED. NO REPRODUCTION IN ANY FORM.

ARROW AIRLINES - APW
1947 - 1954 AND 1980 - PRESENT
INTERNATIONAL CHARTER
- CHANGED NAME FROM ARROW AIRWAYS IN 1983

APW-15W
81MM BRITE GOLDTONE WITH
"AA" AND ARROW ON RED SHIELD

APW-22W
80MM SATIN/BRITE GOLDTONE
WITH WHITE "A" ON RED CIRCLE

APW-30W
80MM SATIN/BRITE GOLDTONE RED "A" IN CENTER

ASPEN AIRWAYS - APX
1962 - 1991
ROCKY MT AREA - WEST COAST US
- STARTED AIR TAXI OPERATIONS IN 1953
- ROUTES PURCHASED BY MESA AIRLINES IN 1990
- ROUTES PURCHASED BY AIR WISCONSIN IN 1991

APX-10B
BRITE SILVERTONE

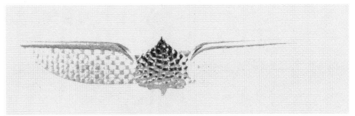

APX-10W
74MM BRITE SILVERTONE

© PHILIP R. MARTIN 1995 ALL RIGHTS RESERVED. NO REPRODUCTION IN ANY FORM.

ATLANTA EXPRESS - AXP
1982 - 1983
US COMMUTER AND CARGO
• MERGED WITH SUNBIRD AIRLINES IN 1983

AXP-10W
77MM FLAT SILVERTONE

AXP-15W
77MM FLAT SILVERTONE

AXP-20B
SATIN / BRITE GOLDTONE WITH RED CENTER

AXP-20W
77MM SATIN / BRITE
GOLDTONE WITH RED CENTER

AXP-25W
77MM SATIN / BRITE
GOLDTONE WITH RED CENTER

ATLANTIC AIRWAYS - ATL
1941 - 1942
ATLANTIC SERVICE WW2
• A JOINT TRANSATLANTIC FERRYING VENTURE BETWEEN PAN
AMERICAN AND BOAC
• EVOLVED INTO ATC AND PAN AM FERRIES

NATM/P

© PHILIP R. MARTIN 1995 ALL RIGHTS RESERVED. NO REPRODUCTION IN ANY FORM.

ATLANTIC COASTAL AIRLINES - ACL
1995 - PRESENT
EAST COAST US
• NEW REGIONAL COMMUTER AIRLINE

ACL-25W
82MM SATIN SILVERTONE

ATLANTIC SOUTHEAST AIRLINES - ASE
1979 - PRESENT
SOUTH US
• WORKS AS A COMMUTER WITH DELTA AIRLINES

ASE-20W
85MM SATIN / BRITE SILVERTONE WITH RED LETTERS

ASE-22W
85MM SATIN / BRITE SILVERTONE WITH RED LETTERS

AV AIR (SEE AIR VIRGINIA LISTING)

© PHILIP R. MARTIN 1995 ALL RIGHTS RESERVED. NO REPRODUCTION IN ANY FORM.

ALASKA AIRLINES

Serving the Top of the World

GENERAL OFFICES: ANCHORAGE, ALASKA

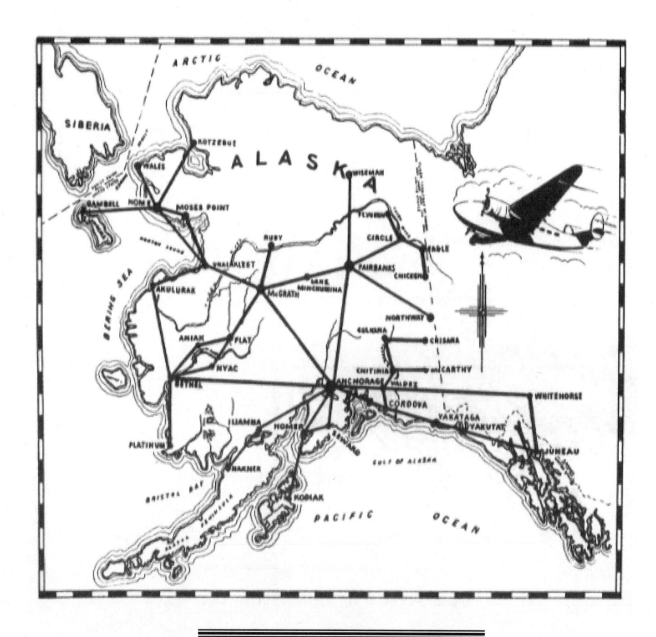

B

BAR HARBOR AIRLINES - BAR
1952 - 1992
NORTHEAST US COMMUTER OPERATIONS
• STARTED SCHEDULED OPERATIONS IN 1968

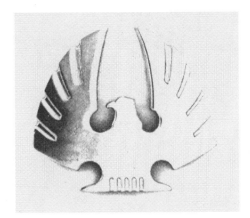

BAR-10B
BRITE/SATIN SILVERTONE

BAR-10W
84MM BRITE/SATIN SILVERTONE

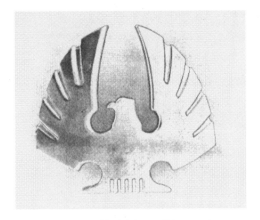

BAR-20B
BRITE/SATIN GOLDTONE

BAR-20W
84MM BRITE/SATIN GOLDTONE

BERING AIRLINES - BRE
1979 - PRESENT
ALASKAN REGIONAL COMMUTER
• OPERATES AS AN ALASKA AIRLINES COMMUTER

NATM/P

© PHILIP R. MARTIN 1995 ALL RIGHTS RESERVED. NO REPRODUCTION IN ANY FORM.

BIG SKY AIRLINES - BSY
1978 - PRESENT
NORTH CENTRAL US REGIONAL COMMUTER
• OPERATES PRIMARILY OUT OF MONTANA

BSY-10W
80MM SATIN/BRITE GOLDTONE
WITH BLUE LOGO IN THE CENTER

BSY-12W
80MM SATIN/BRITE GOLDTONE
WITH BLUE LOGO IN THE CENTER

BOEING AIR TRANSPORT - BOI
1927 - 1931
WEST TO MID-WEST MAIL RUN
• CHANGED NAME TO UNITED AIR LINES IN 1931

NATM/P

BOEING AIRCRAFT INC. - BOE
1930 - PRESENT
INTERNATIONAL
• AIRCRAFT MANUFACTURER

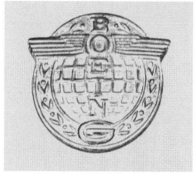

BOE-20B
BRITE GOLDTONE

BOE-20W
81MM BRITE GOLDTONE

BOE-10B and BOE-10W are virtually identical to the above shown except they are sterling.

© PHILIP R. MARTIN 1995 ALL RIGHTS RESERVED. NO REPRODUCTION IN ANY FORM.

BONANZA AIRLINES - BNZ
1949 - 1968
WESTERN US

- MERGED INTO AIR WEST IN 1968

BNZ-10W
89MM BRITE GOLDTONE,
ORANGE & BLACK LOGO CENTER
1949 - 1957

BNZ-12W
89MM BRITE GOLDTONE,
ORANGE & BLACK LOGO CENTER
1949 - 1957

BNZ-15W
89MM BRITE GOLDTONE WITH ORANGE & BLACK LOGO CENTER
1949 - 1957

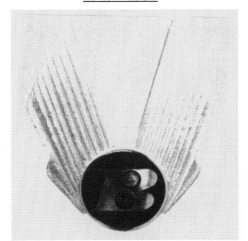

BNZ-20B
SATIN SILVERTONE WITH "B" LOGO ON BLACK CENTER
1958 - 1968

© PHILIP R. MARTIN 1995 ALL RIGHTS RESERVED. NO REPRODUCTION IN ANY FORM.

BNZ-20W
76MM SATIN SILVERTONE
WITH "B" LOGO ON BLACK CENTER
<u>1958 - 1968</u>

BNZ-22W
76MM SATIN SILVERTONE
WITH "B" LOGO ON BLACK CENTER
<u>1958 - 1968</u>

BNZ-25W
76MM SATIN SILVERTONE WITH "B" LOGO ON BLACK CENTER
<u>1958 - 1968</u>

BOSTON-MAINE AIRWAYS - BOS
1931 - 1937

NORTHEAST US
- ACQUIRED NATIONAL AIRWAYS IN 1937
- RENAMED NORTHEAST AIRLINES IN 1940

NATM/P

BOWEN AIRLINES - BOW
1933 - 1936

TEXAS
- OUT OF BUSINESS IN 1936

NATM/P

© PHILIP R. MARTIN 1995 ALL RIGHTS RESERVED. NO REPRODUCTION IN ANY FORM.

BRANIFF AIRLINES - BRA
1984 - 1989
US
• SECOND ATTEMPT TO RESURECT AIRLINE FAILED IN 1989

BRA-10W
86MM FLAT SILVERTONE

BRA-15W
86MM FLAT SILVERTONE

BRANIFF AIRWAYS - BRN
1932 - 1947
MID-WEST US
• CHANGED NAME TO "INTERNATIONAL AIRLINES"

BRN-10W
73MM SATIN GOLDTONE, EARLY LOGO IN CENTER

BRANIFF EXPRESS- BXP

1986 - 1989
REGIONAL COMMUTER AIRLINES CONSISTING OF :
• ALTUS AIRLINES, OKLAHOMA FROM 1987
• CAPITOL AIR LINES, KANSAS FROM 1986
• MID CONTINENT AIRLINES FROM 1987

© PHILIP R. MARTIN 1995 ALL RIGHTS RESERVED. NO REPRODUCTION IN ANY FORM.

BRANIFF INTERNATIONAL AIRLINES - BRF
1947 - 1982
INTERNATIONAL

- FOUNDED BY BROTHERS PAUL AND TOM BRANIFF AS BRANIFF AIRWAYS
- MERGED WITH MID-CONTINENT AIRLINES IN 1952
- BOUGHT PAN-AMERICAN GRACE AIRWAYS IN 1967
- DECLARED BANKRUPTCY IN 1982

BRF-10B
NATM • SATIN GOLDTONE WITH
RED & BLUE ENAMELING
1950 - 1967

BRF-10W
91MM SATIN GOLDFILLED
OR GOLDTONE
1950 - 1967

BRF-12W
91MM SATIN GOLDFILLED
OR GOLDTONE
1950 - 1967

BRF-20B
BRITE GOLDTONE /
WHITE CENTER
1967 - 1978

© PHILIP R. MARTIN 1995 ALL RIGHTS RESERVED. NO REPRODUCTION IN ANY FORM.

BRF-20W
87MM BRITE GOLDTONE,
WHITE CENTER
<u>1967 - 1978</u>

BRF-22W
87MM BRITE GOLDTONE,
WHITE CENTER
<u>1967 - 1978</u>

BRF-34W
75MM TAN CLOTH WITH
SILVER THREAD
<u>1967 - 1978</u>

BRF-40W
87MM BRITE SILVERTONE
WITH A WHITE CENTER
<u>1978 - 1982</u>

BRF-42W
87MM BRITE SILVERTONE
WITH A WHITE CENTER
<u>1978 - 1982</u>

BRF-44W
75MM BLACK CLOTH WITH
SILVER THREAD
<u>1978 - 1982</u>

© PHILIP R. MARTIN 1995 ALL RIGHTS RESERVED. NO REPRODUCTION IN ANY FORM.

BRANIFF AIRLINES - BRE
1990
SW US
- THIS WAS THE THIRD ATTEMPT TO REVIVE BRANIFF AS A VIABLE CARRIER
- PROMOTERS HAD WINGS PRODUCED BEFORE EVEN ONE AIRCRAFT FLEW
- THE AIRLINE NEVER DID FLY

BRE-30W
87MM BRITE GOLDTONE
WITH A DARK CENTER

BRE-32W
87MM BRITE GOLDTONE
WITH A DARK CENTER

BRITT AIR - BTA
1956 - 1991
REGIONAL COMMUTER OPERATOR

- OPERATED AS CONTINENTAL EXPRESS
- OUT OF BUSINESS IN 1991

BTA-10W
NATM • FLAT SILVERTONE WITH ORANGE LETTERS ON BLUE CENTER

BROCKWAY AIR (NY) - BRY
1988 - 1991
NORTHEAST US COMMUTER
- PURCHASED BY METRO AIRLINES IN 1988
- BECAME METRO NORTHEAST IN MERGER WITH BROCKWAY (VT) IN 1990
- CEASED OPERATIONS IN 1991

NATM/P

© PHILIP R. MARTIN 1995 ALL RIGHTS RESERVED. NO REPRODUCTION IN ANY FORM.

BROCKWAY AIR (VT) - BRT
1990 - 1991
NORTHEAST US COMMUTER
- STARTED AS AIR NORTH
- BECAME METRO NORTHEAST IN MERGER WITH BROCKWAY (NY) IN 1990
- CEASED OPERATIONS IN 1991

NATM/P

BUFFALO AIRWAYS - BUF
1982 - PRESENT
SOUTHERN US REGIONAL CARRIER
- OPERATES AS A BURLINGTON AIR EXPRESS CARRIER

BUF-10B
SATIN GOLDTONE

BUF-10W
87MM SATIN GOLDTONE

BUF-12W
87MM SATIN GOLDTONE

BUF-15W
87MM SATIN GOLDTONE

© PHILIP R. MARTIN 1995 ALL RIGHTS RESERVED. NO REPRODUCTION IN ANY FORM.

BURDETT AIR LINES - BUR
19 XX - 19XX
UNKNOWN

S..D..A..M..

BUR-10W
80MM STERLING WITH BLUE LETTERING

===

BURLINGTON AIR EXPRESS - BAX
19 XX - PRESENT
NATIONAL AIR FREIGHT COMPANY
• CONTRACTS WITH THE FOLLOWING :
• AMRIJET INTERNATIONAL
• BUFFALO AIRWAYS
• JET EAST
• ORION AIR
• ROSENBALM AVIATION
• SOUTHERN AIR TRANSPORT
• SPIRIT OF AMERICA AIRLINES

NATM/P

C

CABLE COMMUTER AIRLINES - CAB
1966 - 1969
SOUTHERN CALIFORNIA - ARIZONA
• MERGED WITH AERO COMMUTER IN 1969 TO FORM GOLDEN WEST AIRLINES

CAB-10W
74MM SATIN GOLDTONE WITH LIGHT GREEN CENTER & GOLD LETTERS

CALIFORNIA CENTRAL AIRLINES - CLC
1947 - 1954
CALIFORNIA CORRIDOR
• DECLARED BANKRUPTCY IN 1953

NATM/P

CALIFORNIA EASTERN AVIATION - CLE
1946 - 1948
TRANSCONTINENTAL AIR CARGO
• CEASED OPERATIONS AND SOLD ASSETS TO SLICK AVIATION IN 1948

CLE-10W
64MM STERLING WITH LIGHT GREEN GLOBE,
BLUE CIRCLE & WHITE FIGURE

© PHILIP R. MARTIN 1995 ALL RIGHTS RESERVED. NO REPRODUCTION IN ANY FORM.

CAPE COD AIRWAY - COD
1933
NEW ENGLAND
• CEASED OPERATIONS IN 1933

NATM/P

CAPITAL AIRLINES - CAP
1948 - 1961
US DOMESTIC
• WAS PENN CENTRAL AIRLINES - RENAMED IN 1948
• MERGED INTO UNITED AIRLINES IN 1961

CAP-10B
SATIN GOLDTONE

CAP-10W
73MM SATIN GOLDTONE

CAP-20B
SATIN GOLDTONE

CAP-20W
86MM SATIN GOLDTONE

© PHILIP R. MARTIN 1995 ALL RIGHTS RESERVED. NO REPRODUCTION IN ANY FORM.

CAPITOL AIRLINES - CPA
1955 - 1989
MIDWEST US REGIONAL COMMUTER
- OPERATED AS A BRANIFF EXPRESS COMMUTER
- OUT OF BUSINESS IN 1989

CPA-10W
73MM BRITE/SATIN SILVERTONE WITH BLUE LETTERING

CAPITOL AIRWAYS - CPO
1928 - 1967
AIR CARGO CARRIER
- ADDED "INTERNATIONAL" IN 1967 (See Next Listing)

CP0-10W
84MM FLAT SILVERTONE

CAPITOL INTERNATIONAL AIRLINES - CPI
1967 - 1984
US - INTERNATIONAL
- OUT OF BUSINESS IN 1984

CPI-10W
82MM SATIN SILVERTONE WITH BLUE "C" AT BOTTOM

© PHILIP R. MARTIN 1995 ALL RIGHTS RESERVED. NO REPRODUCTION IN ANY FORM.

CARNIVAL AIRLINES - CKW
1988 - PRESENT
SOUTHEAST US & CARRIBEAN REGIONAL CARRIER
• NOT AFFLIATED WITH CARNIVAL CRUISE LINES

Peters   Peters

CKW-10B
BRITE/SATIN RED,WHITE
& BLUE CENTER LOGO

CKW-10W
74MM BRITE/SATIN,
RED,WHITE & BLUE CENTER LOGO

Peters   Peters

CKW-12W
74MM BRITE/SATIN,
RED,WHITE & BLUE CENTER LOGO

CKW-15W
74MM BRITE/SATIN,
RED,WHITE & BLUE CENTER LOGO

CASCADE AIRWAYS - CSD
1969 - 1986
NORTHWEST US REGIONAL CARRIER
• OUT OF BUSINESS IN 1986

CSD-10W
89MM BRITE/SATIN SILVERTONE, BLACK SEMI-CIRCLE AND CENTER

© PHILIP R. MARTIN 1995 ALL RIGHTS RESERVED. NO REPRODUCTION IN ANY FORM.

CSD-20W
89MM BRITE/SATIN SILVERTONE

CASINO EXPRESS AIRLINES - CSX
1989 - PRESENT
WESTERN US REGIONAL CARRIER

CPO-10B
SATIN GOLDTONE WITH GREEN
and RED POINT HIGHLIGHTS

CPO-10W
84MM SATIN GOLDTONE WITH
GREEN and RED POINT HIGHLIGHTS

CPO-12W
84MM SATIN GOLDTONE WITH
GREEN and RED POINT HIGHLIGHTS

CPO-15W
84MM SATIN GOLDTONE WITH
GREEN and RED POINT HIGHLIGHTS

© PHILIP R. MARTIN 1995 ALL RIGHTS RESERVED. NO REPRODUCTION IN ANY FORM.

CATALINA AIR LINES - CTL
1953 - 1955
LONG BEACH - AVALON
• CEASED OPERATIONS IN 1955

NATM/P

CATALINA AIRLINES - CAT
1955 - 1959
LONG BEACH - CATALINA ISLAND
• DIFFERENT COMPANY THAN PREVIOUS LISTING • CEASED OPERATIONS IN 1959

NATM/P

CATALINA AIRLINES - CTR
1963 - 1967
LONG BEACH - AVALON
• MERGED INTO AERO COMMUTER IN 1967

NATM/P

CATALINA AIR TRANSPORT - CTT
1940 - 1946
LONG BEACH - CATALINA
• MERGED INTO UNITED AIRLINES IN 1946

NATM/P

CATALINA AMPHIBIOUS TRANSPORT - CAM
1980 - 1982
LONG BEACH - CATALINA COMUTTER
• OUT OF BUSINESS IN JANUARY 1982

CAM-10W
66MM SATIN SILVERTONE

C C AIR - CCA
1979 - PRESENT
EAST COAST US COMMUTER
• CHANGED NAME FROM SUNBIRD AIRLINES IN 1987
• US AIR EXPRESS COMMUTER
• CHAPTER 11 IN 1990

CCA-10W
85MM BRITE / SATIN SILVERTONE WITH DARK BLUE CENTER

CCA-20B
BLACK CLOTH WITH SILVER
BULLION AND METAL CENTER

CCA-22W
87MM BLACK CLOTH WITH SILVER
BULLION AND METAL CENTER

CENTRAL AIRLINES - CTA
1928 - 1929
MID-WEST US
• INTO UNIVERSAL AIR LINES IN 1929

NATM/P

© PHILIP R. MARTIN 1995 ALL RIGHTS RESERVED. NO REPRODUCTION IN ANY FORM.

CENTRAL AIRLINES - CNT
1931 - 1967
MID-WEST US
• INTO FRONTIER AIRLINES IN 1967

Koran

CNT-10W
NATM • STERLING

CNT-22W **CNT-32W**
74MM STERLING 84MM STERLING

CENTURY AIR LINES - CEN
1931 - 1932
MID-WEST US
• SOLD TO AVCO (AMERICAN AIRLINES) IN 1932

NATM/P

CENTURY PACIFIC LINES LTD. - CNP
1931 - 1932
PACIFIC COAST-CALIFORNIA
• SOLD TO AVCO (AMERICAN AIRLINES) IN 1932

NATM/P

© PHILIP R. MARTIN 1995 ALL RIGHTS RESERVED. NO REPRODUCTION IN ANY FORM.

CHALK'S FLYING SERVICE - CHK
1918 - PRESENT
FLORIDA-CARRIBEAN
• CLAIMS TO BE OLDEST CONTINUOUSLY OPERATED CARRIER IN THE WORLD

CHK-30W
73MM BRITE / SATIN GOLDTONE

CHK-42W
79MM BRITE / SATIN GOLDTONE

CHALLENGER AIRLINES - CHL
1946 - 1950
COLORADO, MONTANA, UTAH AND WYOMING
•MERGED INTO FRONTIER AIRLINES IN 1950

NATM/P

CHAPARRAL AIRLINES - CPL
1976 - PRESENT
SOUTHERN US COMMUTER
• SEPERATE SUBSIDIARY OF METRO AIRLINES
• AMERICAN EAGLE COMMUTER

Koran

CPL-10W
NATM • BRITE / SATIN GOLDTONE

© PHILIP R. MARTIN 1995 ALL RIGHTS RESERVED. NO REPRODUCTION IN ANY FORM.

CPL-20B
SATIN / FLAT SILVERTONE

CPL-20W
79 MM SATIN / FLAT SILVERTONE

CHAUTAUQUA AIRLINES - CHQ
1974 - PRESENT
EASTERN US COMMUTER
• LINKED WITH ALLEGHENY COMMUTER

NATM/P

CHICAGO & SOUTHERN AIRLINES - CSO
1934 - 1953
MIDWEST US
• MERGED INTO DELTA IN 1953

CSO-10W
NATM • GOLDTONE WITH BLUE & ORANGE SIDE PANELS

CSO-20B
GOLD FILLED

CSO-20W
82MM GOLD FILLED

© PHILIP R. MARTIN 1995 ALL RIGHTS RESERVED. NO REPRODUCTION IN ANY FORM.

CSO-22W
82MM GOLD FILLED

CSO-25W
82MM GOLD FILLED

CHRISTMAN AIR SYSTEM - CAS
1977 - PRESENT
EAST AND MIDWEST US COMMUTER
• BASED IN PENNSLYVANIA

CAS-10W
71MM BRITE SILVERTONE WITH BLUE "C" ON WHITE CENTER DISC

CIRCLE RAINBOW AIR - CRA
1972 - PRESENT
HAWAIIAN ISLAND COMMUTER

CRA-10W
79MM SATIN GOLDTONE WITH PINK, BLUE & GREEN RAINBOW

© PHILIP R. MARTIN 1995 ALL RIGHTS RESERVED. NO REPRODUCTION IN ANY FORM.

CIVIL AERONAUTICS AUTHORITY - CAA
1938 - 1959
- BECAME CIVIL AERONAUTICS BOARD (CAB) IN 1940
- EVOLVED INTO FEDERAL AVIATION AGENCY (FAA) IN 1959

CAA-10W
76MM STERLING

CAA-14W
76MM GOLD OVER STERLING

CAA-20B
STERLING - WORLD WAR 2 ERA

CAA-20W
76MM STERLING - WORLD WAR 2 ERA

CAA-30B
STERLING - WORLD WAR 2 ERA

CAA-30W
76MM STERLING - WORLD WAR 2 ERA

© PHILIP R. MARTIN 1995 ALL RIGHTS RESERVED. NO REPRODUCTION IN ANY FORM.

COASTAL AIRWAYS - SQV
1975 - 1990
PACIFIC NORTHWEST COMMUTER
- SHUT DOWN OPERATIONS IN 1990

SQV-12W
75MM BRITE SILVERTONE

COLGAN AIRLINES - CLG
1991 - PRESENT
EASTERN US COMMUTER
- STARTED AS NATIONAL CAPITAL AIRWAYS

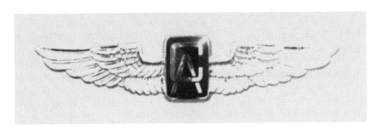

CLG-10W
75MM BRITE SILVERTONE & DARK BLUE BACKGROUND

COLONIAL AIRLINES - COL
1934 - 1956
US/INTERNATIONAL
- ORIGINALLY CANADIAN COLONIAL AIRLINES • CHANGED NAME IN 1942
- MERGED INTO EASTERN AIR LINES IN 1956

COL-10W
87MM SATIN GOLDTONE, RED, WHITE & BLUE CENTER

© PHILIP R. MARTIN 1995 ALL RIGHTS RESERVED. NO REPRODUCTION IN ANY FORM.

COLONIAL AIR TRANSPORT - CLT
1926 - 1929
NORTHEAST US
• INTO AMERICAN AIRWAYS

NATM/P

COLORADO AIRWAYS - CBU
1926 - 1927
ROCKY MOUNTAIN REGION
• MERGED INTO WESTERN AIR EXPRESS IN 1927

NATM/P

COLUMBIA AIRLINES - CLU
1935 - 1936
MID-WEST US
• CEASED OPERATIONS IN 1936

NATM/P

COMAIR - COM
1976 - PRESENT
MIDWEST US REGIONAL COMMUTER

COM-10W
75MM BRITE SILVERTONE
WITH RED CENTER

COM-15W
75MM BRITE SILVERTONE
WITH RED CENTER

© PHILIP R. MARTIN 1995 ALL RIGHTS RESERVED. NO REPRODUCTION IN ANY FORM.

COMBS AIRWAYS - CBZ
1957 - 1984
WESTERN & MIDWEST US REGIONAL
- OUT OF BUSINESS IN 1984

CBZ-10W
78MM BRITE SILVERTONE, BLUE CENTER

COMMAND AIRWAYS - CMM
1966 - 1991
NORTHEAST US COMMUTER
- PART OF THE AMERICAN EAGLE COMMUTER SYSTEM
- MERGED INTO FLAGSHIP AIRLINES IN 1991

CMM-10W
72MM STERLING WITH VERTICAL RED "C" AND BLUE "A"

COMMUTER AIRLINES - CMU
1964 - 1991
EAST COAST COMMUTER
- OUT OF BUSINESS IN 1991

NATM/P

© PHILIP R. MARTIN 1995 ALL RIGHTS RESERVED. NO REPRODUCTION IN ANY FORM.

CON0CO **(CONTINENTAL OIL COMPANY)** - CON
1949 - PRESENT
US & WORLDWIDE
- CORPORATE AIRCRAFT OPERATIONS

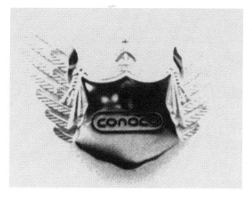

CON-30B
BRITE GOLDTONE,
BLACK LETTERING

CON-30W
72MM BRITE GOLDTONE,
BLACK LETTERING

CONSOLIDATED VULTEE AIRLINES - CAC
1942 - 1945
AIRLINE CREATED BY AIRCRAFT MANUFACTURER KNOWN AS "CORSAIRWAY"
- CEASED AIRLINE OPERATIONS PRIOR TO THE END OF WW2

CAC-10B
STERLING WITH
BLACK LETTERING

CAC-12W
75MM STERLING WITH GOLDTONE AND
BLACK LETTERING

© PHILIP R. MARTIN 1995 ALL RIGHTS RESERVED. NO REPRODUCTION IN ANY FORM.

CONQUEST AIRLINES - CAC
1986 - 1988
SOUTHERN US REGIONAL COMMUTER
• OUT OF BUSINESS IN 1988

NATM/P

CONTINENTAL AIRLINES - CTI
1928
US
• MERGED INTO UNIVERSAL AIRLINES SAME YEAR

NATM/P

CONTINENTAL AIR LINES - COA
1937 - PRESENT
US & INTERNATIONAL CARRIER
• EVOLVED FROM VARNEY AIR TRANSPORT(SW) IN 1937
• ABSORBED FRONTIER AIRLINES IN 1986
• MERGED WITH TEXAS INTERNATIONAL AIRWAYS IN 1982
• ACQUIRED PEOPLES' EXPRESS IN 1987
• DECLARED CHAPTER 11 IN 1990 • OUT OF CHAPTER 11 IN 1993

COA-20W
81MM BLACK CLOTH WITH GOLD
BULLION & RED, WHITE & BLUE
CENTER - "T-BIRD"
<u>1940 - 1957</u>

COA-25W
81MM BLACK CLOTH WITH GOLD
BULLION & RED, WHITE & BLUE
CENTER - "T-BIRD"
<u>1940 - 1957</u>

© PHILIP R. MARTIN 1995 ALL RIGHTS RESERVED. NO REPRODUCTION IN ANY FORM.

COA-30W
80MM BLACK CLOTH WITH GOLD
BULLION & GOLD/SILVER CENTER
- "T-BIRD"
<u>1957 - 1967</u>

COA-35W
80MM BLACK CLOTH WITH GOLD
BULLION & GOLD/SILVER CENTER
- "T-BIRD"
<u>1957 - 1967</u>

COA-45W
77MM BLACK CLOTH WITH GOLD BULLION
<u>1967 - 1972</u>

COA-50W
87MM BLACK CLOTH WITH GOLD
BULLION & GOLD METAL LOGO
<u>1972 - 1982</u>

COA-55W
87MM BLACK CLOTH WITH GOLD
BULLION & GOLD METAL LOGO
<u>1972 - 1982</u>

© PHILIP R. MARTIN 1995 ALL RIGHTS RESERVED. NO REPRODUCTION IN ANY FORM.

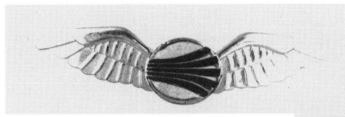

COA-60W
84MM GOLDTONE - "MEATBALL"
<u>1982 - PRESENT</u>

COA-65W
84MM GOLDTONE - "MEATBALL"
<u>1982 - PRESENT</u>

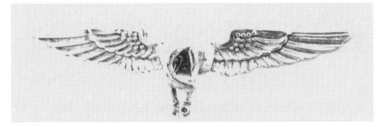

COA-70W
71MM GOLDTONE "HORSE'S ASS" • USED AFTER 1983 STRIKE TO QUIETLY IDENTIFY "SCAB" PILOTS BY REPLACING THEIR COMPANY WINGS WITH THESE WHILE THEIR COATS WERE REMOVED ON THE FLIGHT DECK

COA-80B
BRITE GOLDTONE - 1996 ISSUE

COA-80W
82MM BRITE GOLDTONE - 1996 ISSUE

COA-85W
82MMBRITE GOLDTONE - 1996 ISSUE

© PHILIP R. MARTIN 1995 ALL RIGHTS RESERVED. NO REPRODUCTION IN ANY FORM.

CONTINENTAL AIR SERVICE - CTS
1965 - 1975
SOUTHEAST ASIA
• FOUNDED AS A SUBSIDIARY OF CONTINENTAL AIR LINES
• OPERATED AS A CIA CONTRACT AIRLINE • CEASED OPERATIONS IN 1975

CTS-10W
52MM STERLING

CONTINENTAL AIR TRANSPORT, INC. - CRT
19 XX -19 XX

NATM/P

CONTINENTAL EXPRESS - CXP
1937 - PRESENT
CONTINENTAL AIRLINES REGIONAL COMMUTER
SYSTEM CONSISTING OF :
• AIR NEW ORLEANS, LOUISIANA FROM 1986
• BRITT AIRWAYS, INDIANA FROM 1987
• PROVINCETOWN-BOSTON AIRLINES FROM 1987
• ROCKY MOUNTAIN AIRWAYS, COLORADO FROM 1986
• SOUTHERN JERSEY AIRWAYS, NJ FROM 1988
• TRANS-COLORADO AIRLINES, CO FROM 1986

CORDOVA AIRLINES - COR
1936 - 1967
ALASKA
• MERGED INTO ALASKA AIRLINES IN 1967

NATM/P

CROWN AIRWAYS - CRO
19XX - PRESENT
PUERTO RICO ALLEGHENY COMMUTER
• ORIGINALLY DORADO AIRWAYS

NATM/P

© PHILIP R. MARTIN 1995 ALL RIGHTS RESERVED. NO REPRODUCTION IN ANY FORM.

D

DELTA AIR LINES - DAL
1934 - PRESENT
NATIONAL AND INTERNATIONAL
MERGED WITH:
- CHICAGO & SOUTHERN AIRLINES IN 1953
- NORTHEAST AIRLINES IN 1972
- WESTERN AIRLINES IN 1986

DAL-10W (see **USM-10W**)
GOLD OR GOLDTONE OR
STERLING "US AIRMAIL"
<u>1934-1940</u>

DAL-20W
86MM BLACK CLOTH WITH
SILVER BULLION & BLUE TRIANGLE
<u>1940-1945</u>

DAL-30W
81MM STERLING
<u>1945-1953</u>

DAL-32W
74MM STERLING
<u>1945-1953</u>

© PHILIP R. MARTIN 1995 ALL RIGHTS RESERVED. NO REPRODUCTION IN ANY FORM.

DAL-40B
SATIN GOLDTONE WITH
"RED BALL" CENTER,
GOLD DELTA C & S
<u>1953-1956</u>

DAL-40W
84MM SATIN GOLDTONE
WITH "RED BALL" CENTER,
GOLD DELTA C & S
<u>1953-1956</u>

DAL-42W
84MM SATIN GOLDTONE, "RED BALL" CENTER, GOLD DELTA C&S
<u>1953-1956</u>

DAL-45W
84MM SATIN GOLDTONE, "RED BALL" CENTER, GOLD DELTA C&S
<u>1953-1956</u>

© PHILIP R. MARTIN 1995 ALL RIGHTS RESERVED. NO REPRODUCTION IN ANY FORM.

DAL-50B
SATIN GOLDTONE WITH "BLUE BALL" CENTER, GOLD "DELTA"
<u>1956-1972</u>

DAL-50W
83MM SATIN GOLDTONE WITH "BLUE BALL" CENTER, GOLD "DELTA"
<u>1956-1972</u>

DAL-52W
83MM SATIN GOLDTONE WITH "BLUE BALL" CENTER, GOLD "DELTA"
<u>1956-1972</u>

DAL-55W
83MM SATIN GOLDTONE WITH "BLUE BALL" CENTER, GOLD "DELTA"
<u>1956-1972</u>

DAL-60W
84MM SATIN GOLDTONE WITH RED, WHITE & BLUE LOGO IN CENTER
<u>1972-PRESENT</u>

DAL-62W
84MM SATIN GOLDTONE WITH RED WHITE & BLUE LOGO IN CENTER
<u>1972-PRESENT</u>

© PHILIP R. MARTIN 1995 ALL RIGHTS RESERVED. NO REPRODUCTION IN ANY FORM.

DAL-65W
84MM SATIN GOLDTONE WITH RED, WHITE & BLUE LOGO IN CENTER
1972-PRESENT

DHL AIRWAYS (DALSEY, HILLBLOOM & LIND) - DHL
1980-PRESENT
INTERNATIONAL AIR CARGO CARRIER

DHL-12W
71MM BRITE GOLDTONE WITH BROWN CENTER

DHL-20B
BRITE GOLDTONE WITH BROWN CENTER

DHL-20W
74MM BRITE GOLDTONE WITH BROWN CENTER

© PHILIP R. MARTIN 1995 ALL RIGHTS RESERVED. NO REPRODUCTION IN ANY FORM.

DIAMOND MATCH CORPORATION - DIA
19XX - PRESENT
MANUFACTURING COMPANY

DIA-10W
61MM FLAT SILVERTONE WITH RED"M" ON WHITE DIAMOND

DISCOVERY AIRLINES - DIS
1989 - 19XX
US COMMUTER
• OUT OF BUSINESS

DIS-10W
71MM SATIN GOLDTONE

© PHILIP R. MARTIN 1995 ALL RIGHTS RESERVED. NO REPRODUCTION IN ANY FORM.

DOLPHIN AIRLINES - DOL
1981 - 1987
SOUTHEAST US-FLORIDA COMMUTER

- CHANGED NAME FROM DOLPHIN AIRWAYS IN 1983
- CEASED OPERATIONS IN 1987

DOL-10W
79MM SATIN SILVERTONE, ORANGE & WHITE CENTER

DOL-12W
79MM SATIN SILVERTONE, ORANGE & WHITE CENTER

DOL-15W
79MM SATIN SILVERTONE WITH ORANGE & WHITE CENTER

© PHILIP R. MARTIN 1995 ALL RIGHTS RESERVED. NO REPRODUCTION IN ANY FORM.

E
EASTERN AIR LINES - EAL
1934 - 1991
INTERNATIONAL

- EVOLVED FROM EASTERN AIR TRANSPORT
- "THE LINDEBERG LINE"
- HEADED BY EDDIE RICKENBACKER FOR A TIME
- DIED A TERRIBLE DEATH AT THE HANDS OF FRANK LORENZO
- BANKRUPT IN 1991

EAL-20B
SILVERTONE WITH RED BIRD
LOGO IN CENTER

EAL-20W
99MM BLACK CLOTH WITH SILVER
BULLION AND RED BIRD LOGO

EAL-25B
GOLDTONE BURST WITH
RED BIRD LOGO

EAL-25W
NATM • GOLDTONE BURST WITH
RED BIRD LOGO IN CENTER

Koran

EAL-35W
NATM • GOLDTONE WITH
GOLDEN EAGLE CENTER

EAL-40W
80MM BRITE/SATIN GOLDTONE
WHITE LOGO ON BLUE CENTER DISC

© PHILIP R. MARTIN 1995 ALL RIGHTS RESERVED. NO REPRODUCTION IN ANY FORM.

EAL-42W
80MM BRITE/SATIN GOLDTONE
WHITE LOGO ON BLUE CENTER

EAL-45W
80MM BRITE/SATIN GOLDTONE
WHITE LOGO ON BLUE CENTER

EASTERN AIR TRANSPORT - EAT
1930 - 1934
- ACQUIRED NEW YORK AIRWAYS IN 1931
- ACQUIRED LUDDINGTON AIRWAYS IN 1934
- CHANGED NAME TO EASTERN AIR LINES WHEN ITS STOCK WAS ACQUIRED BY GENERAL MOTORS

NATM/P

EASTERN EXPRESS - EXP
1989 - 1991
EASTERN US COMMUTER CONSISTING OF :
- AIR MIDWEST AIRLINES, KANSAS FROM 1985
- ATLANTIS AIRLINES, SOUTH CAROLINA FROM 1985
- AVIATION ASSOCIATES, VIRGIN ISLANDS FROM 1985
- BAR HARBOR AIRLINES, MAINE FROM 1986
- LIAT AIRLINES, ANTIGUA FROM 1987
- METRO EXPRESS, GEORGIA FROM 1984
- PRECISION AIRLINES FROM 1986
- SOUTHERN JERSEY AIRWAYS FROM 1988
- • DIED ALONG WITH EASTERN AIRLINES IN 1991

EXP-10B
FLAT SILVERTONE 3 COLOR CENTER

EXP-10W
79MM FLAT SILVERTONE & RED,
WHITE, BLUE CENTER

© PHILIP R. MARTIN 1995 ALL RIGHTS RESERVED. NO REPRODUCTION IN ANY FORM.

ELLIS AIR LINES - ELL
1940 - 1962
ALASKA MAIL ROUTE
• MERGED WITH ALASKA COASTAL AIRLINES IN 1962

NATM/P

EMBRY-RIDDLE AIRLINES - EMB
1927 - 1930
EARLY CINNCINATTI-CHICAGO AIR MAIL
• BOUGHT BY AMERICAN AIRWAYS IN 1950 • CONTINUED ON AS AN AVIATION COLLEGE TO THE PRESENT DAY

NATM/P

EMERY WORLDWIDE (CF) - EWW
19XX - PRESENT
WORLDWIDE AIR CARGO CARRIER

EWW-10W
84MM BRITE/SATIN GOLDTONE
WITH RED AND BLACK LETTERS

EWW-15W
84MM BRITE/SATIN GOLDTONE
WITH RED AND BLACK LETTERS

EWW-20W
78MM FLAT BRONZETONE

EWW-25W
78MM FLAT BRONZETONE

© PHILIP R. MARTIN 1995 ALL RIGHTS RESERVED. NO REPRODUCTION IN ANY FORM.

EMPIRE AIR LINES - EMP
1946 - 1952
SOUTHWESTERN US
• ORIGINALLY ZIMMERLY AIR LINES IN 1944 • MERGED INTO WEST COAST AIRLINES IN 1952

NATM/P

EMPIRE AIR LINES - EMI
19XX - 1984
NORTHEAST US - REGIONAL CARRIER
• MERGED WITH PIEDMONT AIRLINES IN 1984

NATM/P

ERA AVIATION - ERA
1948 - PRESENT
ALASKAN REGIONAL CARRIER
• OPERATES AS AN ALASKA AIRLINE COMMUTER

ERA-30W
70 MM SATIN BRONZETONE, RED "E"

EVERGREEN INTERNATIONAL AIRLINES - EIA
1975 - PRESENT
US AIR CARGO AND CHARTER
• STARTED AFTER ACQUISITION OF JOHNSON INTERN. AIRLINES IN 1975

EIA-10W
82MM FLAT SILVERTONE WITH GREEN & WHITE CENTER

EIA-15B
FLAT SILVERTONE WITH GREEN & WHITE CENTER

EIA-15W
82MM FLAT SILVERTONE WITH GREEN & WHITE CENTER

EXECUTIVE AIR - EXK
1979 - 19XX
CARRIBEAN REGIONAL COMMUTER
• OPERATES AS AN AMERICAN EAGLE COMMUTER

NATM/P

© PHILIP R. MARTIN 1995 ALL RIGHTS RESERVED. NO REPRODUCTION IN ANY FORM.

EXPERIMENTAL AIRCRAFT ASSOCIATION - EAA
19XX - PRESENT
INTERNATIONAL
AIRCRAFT BUILDERS' AND PILOTS' GROUP

EAA -10W
NATM • GOLDTONE WITH WHITE AND BLUE CENTER LOGO

EXPRESS ONE INTERNATIONAL - LHN
1983 - PRESENT
SOUTHWEST US - TEXAS
SUPPLEMENTAL COMMUTER

LHN -10W
NATM • BRONZETONE

© PHILIP R. MARTIN 1995 ALL RIGHTS RESERVED. NO REPRODUCTION IN ANY FORM.

F
FEDERAL EXPRESS - FDX
1972 - PRESENT
INTERNATIONAL AIR CARGO

FDX-10W
76MM BRITE/SATIN SILVERTONE

FDX-20W
82MM BRITE/SATIN SILVERTONE
PURPLE/WHITE/RED LOGO IN CENTER

FDX-30W
91MM SATIN SILVERTONE
PURPLE/WHITE/RED LOGO

FIVE STAR AIRLINES (FSA) - FSA
1985-1987
EAST COAST CHARTER AIRLINE
• MERGED WITH AMERICAN TRANS AIR IN 1987

NATM/P

FLAGSHIP AIRLINES, INC. - FLG
19XX - PRESENT
REGIONAL COMMUTER
• AMERICAN EAGLE COMMUTER

NATM/P

© PHILIP R. MARTIN 1995 ALL RIGHTS RESERVED. NO REPRODUCTION IN ANY FORM.

FLEMING INTERNATIONAL AIRLINES - FLM
1973 -1984
WORLDWIDE AIR CARGO CARRIER
• OUT OF BUSINESS IN 1984

NATM/P

FLORIDA AIRWAYS - FLA
1926-1949
ATLANTIC COAST-FLORIDA
• OUT OF BUSINESS IN 1949

NATM/P

FLYING TIGER LINE (THE) - FTL

1947-1989
INTERNATIONAL AIR CARGO
• FOUNDED AS NATIONAL SKYWAY FREIGHT IN 1945
• CHANGED NAME TO "THE FLYING TIGER LINE " IN 1946

• FOUNDED AS NATIONAL SKYWAY FREIGHT IN 1945
• CHANGED NAME TO "THE FLYING TIGER LINE " IN 1946
• LATER CHANGED NAME AGAIN TO " FLYING TIGERS "
• MERGED OUT OF EXISTENCE INTO FEDERAL EXPRESS IN 1989

FTL-10B
STERLING WITH BLUE CIRLE, RED BANNER & "SHARK'S TEETH"   1947 - 1958

FTL-10W
81MM STERLING WITH RED & BLUE
"SHARK'S TEETH"
1947 - 1957

FTL-12W
81MM STERLING WITH RED &BLUE
"SHARK'S TEETH"
1947 - 1957

© PHILIP R. MARTIN 1995 ALL RIGHTS RESERVED. NO REPRODUCTION IN ANY FORM.

FTL-20B
STERLING WITH "T"- ARROW
IN "SEGMENTED" CIRCLE
<u>1958 - 1977</u>

FTL-20W
STERLING WITH "T"- ARROW
IN "SEGMENTED" CIRCLE
<u>1958 - 1977</u>

FTL-30W
81MM STERLING or FLAT SILVERTONE
WITH TIGER FACE LOGO IN SQUARE
<u>1977 - 1989</u>

FTL-32W
81MM STERLING or FLAT SILVERTONE
WITH TIGER FACE LOGO IN SQUARE
<u>1977 - 1989</u>

FTL-35W
81MM STERLING or FLAT SILVERTONE WITH TIGER FACE LOGO IN SQUARE
<u>1977 - 1989</u>

THE USE OF THE "SEGMENTED" or "SPLIT T" OVERLAPPED WITH THE "TIGER FACE"

© PHILIP R. MARTIN 1995 ALL RIGHTS RESERVED. NO REPRODUCTION IN ANY FORM.

FREEDOM AIRLINES - FRE
1980-1984
MIDWEST- EAST US COMMUTER
• CEASED OPERATIONS IN 1984

NATM/P

FRONTIER AIRLINES - FAL
1950-1986
US

• FOUNDED AS MONARCH AIR LINES IN 1946
• MERGED WITH CHALLENGER AIR LINES IN 1947
• MERGED WITH ARIZONA AIRWAYS IN 1950
• ACQUIRED CENTRAL AIRLINES IN 1967
• PURCHASED OUT OF BANKRUPTCY BY CONTINENTAL AIRLINES IN 1986

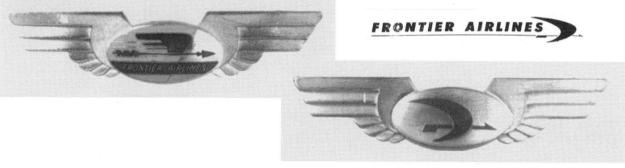

F. Ririe   F. Ririe

FAL-10W
75MM GOLDTONE WITH DARK
RED & GREEN LOGO IN CENTER
1950-1965

FAL-20W
75MM GOLDTONE WITH LIGHT
GREEN LOGO IN CENTER
1965-1976

FAL-35W
82MM SATIN GOLDTONE

1976-1978

FAL-45W
82MM SATIN GOLDTONE
WITH MAROON CENTER
1978-1986

© PHILIP R. MARTIN 1995 ALL RIGHTS RESERVED. NO REPRODUCTION IN ANY FORM.

FAL-52W
81MM SATIN GOLDTONE WITH
MAROON CENTER
<u>1978- 1986</u>

FRONTIER AIRLINES - FRL
1994 - PRESENT
WESTERN US REGIONAL AIRLINE
• OPERATES AIRCRAFT WITH WILDLIFE PAINT SCHEMES

FRL-12W
81MM SATIN SILVERTONE WITH GREEN CENTER

FRL-15W
81MM SATIN SILVERTONE WITH GREEN CENTER

© PHILIP R. MARTIN 1995 ALL RIGHTS RESERVED. NO REPRODUCTION IN ANY FORM.

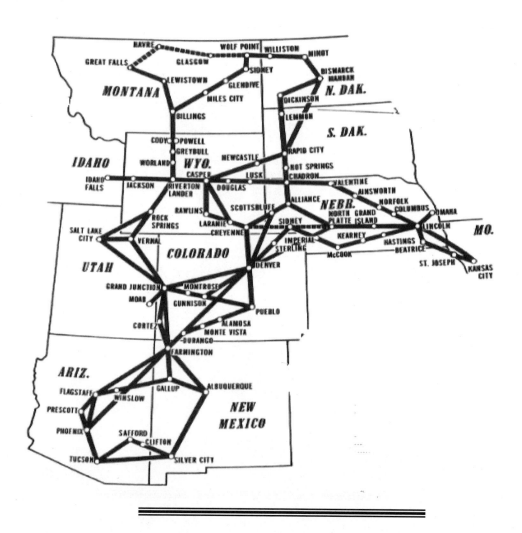

G

GARRETT AIR RESEARCH - GAR
19XX - PRESENT
US
• MAJOR AIRCRAFT ENGINE AND POWERPLANT MANUFACTURER

GAR-10W
81MM FLAT SILVERTONE

GENERAL AIR LINES - GEN
1934
US
• EVOLVED INTO WESTERN AIR EXPRESS IN 1934

S.D.A.M.

GEN-10W
81MM GOLDTONE

GENERAL ELECTRIC CO. - GEE
19XX - PRESENT
INTERNATIONAL ENERGY & MANUFACTURING

GEE-10W
80MM SATIN / BRITE GOLDTONE

© PHILIP R. MARTIN 1995 ALL RIGHTS RESERVED. NO REPRODUCTION IN ANY FORM.

GLOBAL INTERNATIONAL AIRWAYS - GIA
1977 - 1983
US AND WORLDWIDE CHARTER
• BANKRUPT IN 1983

NATM/P

GOLDEN PACIFIC AIRLINES - GPA
1981 - 1986
SOUTHWEST US- ARIZONA- NEVADA COMMUTER

GPA-10W
84MM GREEN CLOTH WITH GOLD BULLION

GOLDEN WEST AIRLINES - GWA
1968 - 1983
CALIFORNIA

• CREATED BY MERGER OF:
  AERO COMMUTER (AERO COMMUTER, CATALINA & AVALON)
  & GOLDEN WEST AIRLINES & SKYMARK AIRLINES & CABLE COMMUTER
• ABSORBED LOS ANGELES AIRWAYS IN 1971
• BANKRUPT IN 1983

GWA-10W
74MM BRITE SILVERTONE WITH
SILVER LETTERS ON A RED CENTER

GWA-15W
74MM BRITE SILVERTONE WITH
SILVER LETTERS ON A RED CENTER

© PHILIP R. MARTIN 1995 ALL RIGHTS RESERVED. NO REPRODUCTION IN ANY FORM.

GOODYEAR - GDY
19XX - PRESENT
US TIRE AND RUBBER MANUFACTURER
• AIRSHIP (BLIMP) OPERATION AT VARIOUS LOCATIONS IN THE US

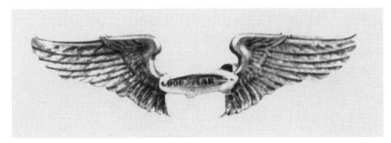

S.D.A.M.

GDY-10W
NATM / STERLING

GRAND CANYON AIRLINES - GYC
1927 - PRESENT
GRAND CANYON SERVICE-ARIZONA

 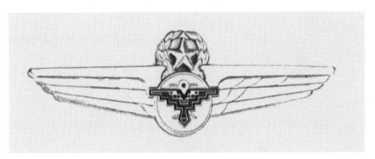

GYC-10B
SATIN GOLDTONE WITH
MULTI COLORED LOGO

GYC-15W
80MM SATIN GOLDTONE WITH
MULTI COLORED LOGO

GREAT AMERICAN AIRWAYS - GAA
1979 - PRESENT
NEVADA BASED REGIONAL CARRIER

NATM/P

© PHILIP R. MARTIN 1995 ALL RIGHTS RESERVED. NO REPRODUCTION IN ANY FORM.

GREAT LAKES AVIATION - GLK
1979 - PRESENT
MIDWEST US COMMUTER

GLK-10B
SILVERTONE WITH RED LETTERS

GLK-10W
75MM SILVERTONE WITH RED LETTERS

GREAT NORTHERN AIRLINES, INC. - GNA
1975 - 1981
ALASKAN REGIONAL AIRLINE
• STARTED AS FAIRBANKS AIR SERVICE IN 1946

NATM/P

GREAT WESTERN AIRLINES - GNA
1968 - 1982
CENTRAL US REGIONAL AIRLINE
• STARTED AS ROSS AVIATION IN 1968

GNA-15W
80 MM SATIN / BRITE GOLDTONE

© PHILIP R. MARTIN 1995 ALL RIGHTS RESERVED. NO REPRODUCTION IN ANY FORM.

GULF AIR LINES - GUL
1928
SE US
• INTO SOUTHERN AIRWAYS (AMERICAN AIRLINES)

NATM/P

GULF COAST AIRLINE (THE) - GLF
1923 - 1933
SOUTHERN US
• ENDED SERVICE IN 1933

NATM/P

GULF AND WESTERN AIRLINE - GLW
19XX - 19XX

NATM/P

H
HANFORD (TRI-STATE) AIR LINES - HAN
1932 - 1952
MID-CONTINENT US
• BECAME MID-CONTINENT AIRLINES IN 1936

NATM/P

HAWAIIAN AIRLINES - HAL
1941 - PRESENT
PACIFIC-US
• EMERGED FROM INTER-ISLAND AIRLINES IN 1941

Koran

HAL-10W
NATM • SILVERTONE WITH RED,
WHITE & ORANGE SHEILD

HAL 20W
78MM BRITE SILVERTONE WITH
RED LOGO & LETTERS ON BLUE SHEILD

HAL 22W
78MM BRITE SILVERTONE WITH
RED LOGO & LETTERS ON BLUE SHEILD

HAL 25W
78MM BRITE SILVERTONE WITH
RED LOGO & LETTERS ON BLUE SHEILD

HAL 30W
73MM BRITE GOLDTONE WITH
RED LOGO & LETTERS ON BLUE SHEILD

HAL 32W
73MM BRITE GOLDTONE WITH RED
LOGO & LETTERS ON BLUE SHEILD

© PHILIP R. MARTIN 1995 ALL RIGHTS RESERVED. NO REPRODUCTION IN ANY FORM.

HAWAIIAN RAINBOW AIR - HRA
1972 - PRESENT
PACIFIC COMMUTER

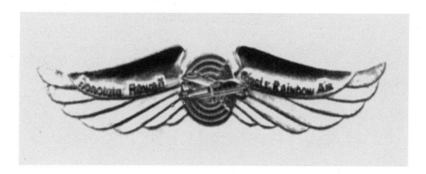

HRA-10W
83MM SATIN GOLDTONE WITH PASTEL COLORED RAINBOW CENTER
NAME PRINTED ACROSS THE WINGS

HENSON AIRLINES - HEN
1931 - PRESENT
NORTHEAST US COMMUTER
- BECAME PASSENGER CARRYING IN 1962
- PIEDMONT REGIONAL COMMUTER IN 1983
- CURRENTLY US AIR EXPRESS SINCE 1989

NATM/P

HORIZON AIRLINES - QXE
1981 - PRESENT
NORTHWEST US REGIONAL COMMMUTER FOR ALASKA AIRLINES
- ABSORBED AIR OREGON IN 1982
- MERGED WITH TRANSWESTERN AIRLINES IN 1983

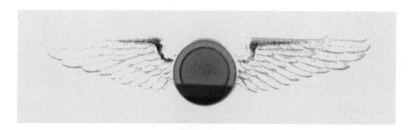

QXE-10W
84MM SATIN GOLDTONE WITH ORANGE, RED & BLUE CENTER

© PHILIP R. MARTIN 1995 ALL RIGHTS RESERVED. NO REPRODUCTION IN ANY FORM.

HUGHES AIR WEST - HAW
1968 - 1980
WESTERN US

- EVOLVED FROM FROM AIR WEST IN 1968
- ABSORBED WEST COAST AIRLINES, PACIFIC AIRLINES & BONANZA AIRLINES IN 1968
- MERGED INTO REPUBLIC AIRLINES IN 1980

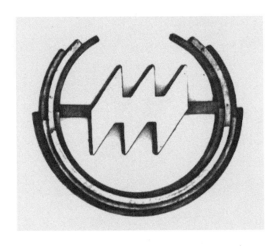

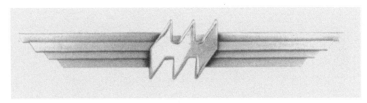

HAW-10B
83MM BRITE/SATIN GOLDTONE

HAW-10W
83MM BRITE/SATIN SILVERTONE

THERE IS AN IDENTICAL SET IN GOLDTONE USED UP TO THE MERGER —
THESE ARE CLASSIFIED AS **HAW-20B** AND **HAW-20W**

I

IMPERIAL AIRLINES - IMP
1967 - 1986
REGIONAL CARRIER - SOUTHERN CALIFORNIA
• FOUNDED AS VISCO FLYING CO. IN 1964 • CHANGED NAME TO
IMPERIAL AIRLINES IN 1967
• OUT OF BUSINESS IN 1986

NATM/P

INLAND AIR LINES - INL
1930 - 1943
WESTERN US
• MERGED INTO WESTERN AIRLINES IN 1944

NATM/P

INTERCONTINENTAL AIRWAYS - INC
19XX - 19XX
UNKNOWN

INC-10W
80MM SATIN/BRITE GOLDTONE
BLUE CENTER WITH HEMISPHERE

INTER-ISLAND AIRWAYS - INI
1929 - 1941
HAWAII-PACIFIC
• CHANGED NAME INTO HAWAIIAN AIRLINES IN 1941

NATM/P

© PHILIP R. MARTIN 1995 ALL RIGHTS RESERVED. NO REPRODUCTION IN ANY FORM.

INTERMOUNTAIN AIRWAYS - INM
19XX - 1978
ROCKY MOUNTAIN COMMUTER AND AIR CARGO
• ABSORBED BY ROCKY MOUNTAIN AIRWAYS IN 1978

NATM/P

INTERSTATE AIRLINES - INS
1928 - 1929
MID-WEST US
• EVOLVED INTO AVCO (AMERICAN AIRLINES) IN 1929

NATM/P

INTERSTATE AIRLINES - IST
1978 - PRESENT
MIDWEST US CHARTER CARRIER

S.D.A.M.

IST-12W
80MM BRITE SILVERTONE WITH BLACK LETTERS IN WHITE CIRCLE

IST-22W
80MM BRITE/SATIN SILVERTONE RED, WHITE & BLUE LOGO WHITE CENTER

© PHILIP R. MARTIN 1995 ALL RIGHTS RESERVED. NO REPRODUCTION IN ANY FORM.

J

JET AMERICA AIRLINES - JAM
1981 - 1987
US SCHEDULED PASSENGER SERVICE
• PURCHASED BY ALASKA AIRLINES IN 1987

JAM-10B
BRITE GOLDTONE, BLACK LOGO

JAM-10W
75MM BRITE GOLDTONE, BLACK LOGO

JET EAST INTERNATIONAL - JED
19XX - PRESENT
NATIONAL & INTERNATIONAL JET CHARTER
• CHANGED NAME TO EXPRESS ONE IN 1987

NATM/P

JETSTREAM INTERNATIONAL AIRLINES - JIA
1988 - PRESENT
MID-WEST US
• OPERATES AS A US AIR COMMUTER

NATM/P

© PHILIP R. MARTIN 1995 ALL RIGHTS RESERVED. NO REPRODUCTION IN ANY FORM.

JET 24 INTERNATIONAL AIRWAYS - JCS
1979 - PRESENT
NATIONAL & INTERNATIONAL JET CHARTER

JCS-10W
72MM BRITE GOLDTONE, BLACK CENTER

JCS-20W
72MM BRITE GOLDTONE, WHITE CENTER

JOHNSON FLYING SERVICE - JFS
19XX - 19XX

JFS-10W
76MM STERLING

JOHNSON INTERNATIONAL AIRLINES - JON
1929 - 1975
US AIR CARGO CARRIER
• EVOLVED INTO EVERGREEN INTERNATIONAL IN 1975

JON-10W
80MM SATIN SILVERTONE WITH RED & BLUE "J" ON WHITE CENTER DISC

© PHILIP R. MARTIN 1995 ALL RIGHTS RESERVED. NO REPRODUCTION IN ANY FORM.

JOLLY VOYAGER AIRWAYS - JOL
19XX - 19XX
INTERNATIONAL TRAVEL CLUB CHARTERS

JOL-10W
78MM BRITE GOLDTONE WITH GOLD LETTERS ON BLACK DISC

Koran

JOL-15W
78MM BRITE GOLDTONE WITH GOLDLETTERS ON BLACK DISC

© PHILIP R. MARTIN 1995 ALL RIGHTS RESERVED. NO REPRODUCTION IN ANY FORM.

K

K-2 AIRLINES - KTO
19XX - PRESENT
ALASKAN REGIONAL COMMUTER

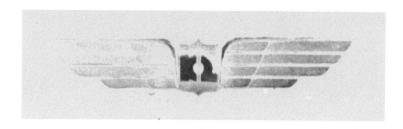

KTO-10W
75MM BRITE/SATIN SILVERTONE

KEY AIRLINES - KEY
1962 - PRESENT
EASTERN US CHARTER
• WORLD AIRWAYS SUBSIDIARY

KEY-10W
77MM BRITE GOLDTONE WITH RED & BLUE ON WHITE FIELD

© PHILIP R. MARTIN 1995 ALL RIGHTS RESERVED. NO REPRODUCTION IN ANY FORM.

KIWI INTERNATIONAL AIRLINES - KIA
1992 - PRESENT
EAST COAST US REGIONAL AIRLINE

KIA-10B
SATIN DARK GOLDTONE WITH WHITE
LOGO ON LIGHT GREEN & VIOLET DISC

KIA-12W
78MM SATIN DARK GOLDTONE
WITH LOGO ON LT. GREEN & VIOLET DISC

KIA-15W
78MM SATIN DARK GOLDTONEWITH WHITE LOGO ON LT GREEN & VIOLET DISC

KODIAK AIRWAYS - KOD
1960 - 1973
ALASKA
• MERGED WITH WESTERN ALASKA AIRLINES TO FORM KODIAK WESTERN ALASKA AIRLINES IN 1973

NATM/P

© PHILIP R. MARTIN 1995 ALL RIGHTS RESERVED. NO REPRODUCTION IN ANY FORM.

KODIAK WESTERN ALASKA AIRLINES - KWA
1973 - 1985
ALASKA
- CREATED FROM MERGER OF KODIAK AIRWAYS AND WESTERN ALASKA AIRLINES IN 1973
- CEASED OPERATIONS IN 1985

NATM/P

KOHLER AVIATION CORP. - KOL
1929 -1934
GREAT LAKES AREA US
- ACQUIRED BY PENNSLYVANIA AIRLINES IN 1934

NATM/P

© PHILIP R. MARTIN 1995 ALL RIGHTS RESERVED. NO REPRODUCTION IN ANY FORM.

L

L.A.B. FLYING SERVICE - LAB
1956 - PRESENT
ALASKAN CHARTER SERVICE
• OPERATES AS AN ALASKA AIRLINES COMMUTER

LAB-10W
82MM GOLDTONE BRITE WING / SATIN CENTER & BLUE LETTERS

LAKE CENTRAL AIRLINES - LAK
1950 - 1966
MID-US
• FOUNDED AS ROSCOE TURNER AERONAUTICAL CORP. IN 1947
• CHANGED NAME TO TURNER AIRLINES IN 1949
• CHANGED NAMED TO LAKE CENTRAL AIRLINES IN 1950
• MERGED INTO ALLEGHENY AIRLINES IN 1966

LAK-10B
BRITE SILVERTONE WITH RED OVAL, SUN, BLACK POLE AND PLANE FIGURE

LAK-10W
75MM BRITE SILVERTONE WITH RED OVAL, SUN, BLACK POLE & AIRPLANE

© PHILIP R. MARTIN 1995 ALL RIGHTS RESERVED. NO REPRODUCTION IN ANY FORM.

LONG AND HARMON AIRLINES - LON
1934 -1935
TEXAS AIRLINE
• MERGED INTO BRANIFF AIRLINES IN 1935

NATM/P

LOS ANGELES AIRWAYS - LAA
1944 -1971
SO CALIFORNIA COMMUTER- HELICOPTERS
• MERGED WITH GOLDEN WEST AIRLINES IN 1971

R. Jones

LAA-10W
NATM • SILVER WITH RED BLUE

LAA-20W
70MM STERLING WITH GREEN LETTERS

LUDINGTON (AIR) LINE - LUD
1929 - 1933
EASTERN US
•MERGED INTO EASTERN (AIR TRANSPORT)AIRLINES IN 1933

NATM/P

M
MACKEY AIRLINES - MAC
1956 - 1967
INTERNATIONAL
• MERGED INTO EASTERN AIRLINES IN 1967

MAC-10W
80MM SATIN/BRITE GOLDTONE BLACK LETTER & TRIANGLE & BLUE LOGO IN A WHITE CIRCLE

MAC-12W
80MM SATIN/BRITE GOLDTONE BLACK LETTER & TRIANGLE & BLUE LOGO IN A WHITE CIRCLE

MADDUX AIR LINES - MAD
1927 - 1930
US

• MERGED INTO TAT IN 1930

C.Weeks

MAD-10W
NATM • SILVERTONE

© PHILIP R. MARTIN 1995 ALL RIGHTS RESERVED. NO REPRODUCTION IN ANY FORM.

MAHALO AIR - MAH
19XX - PRESENT
US - HAWAII COMMUTER

MAH-10W
77MM BRITE/ SATIN GOLDTONE
B. Shuey

MAH-12
77MM BRITE/ SATIN GOLDTONE
B. Shuey

MAMER AIR TRANSPORT - MAM
1929 - 1932
PACIFIC NORTHWEST US
• OUT OF BUSINESS IN 1932

NATM/P

MARK AIR - MRK
1947 - PRESENT
ALASKA & NORTHWEST US

MRK-15W
82MM FLAT SILVERTONE WITH MAROON "M"

© PHILIP R. MARTIN 1995 ALL RIGHTS RESERVED. NO REPRODUCTION IN ANY FORM.

MRK-20W
67MM BRITE SILVERTONE WITH MAROON "MARK"

MARTZ (AIR) - MRZ
1930 - 1932
NEW YORK-PENNSLYVANIA
• MERGED INTO AMERICAN AIRWAYS IN 1932

NATM/P

MARQUETTE AIRLINES - MRQ
1938 - 1941
MID-WEST US
• PURCHASED BY TWA IN 1941

NATM/P

MAYFLOWER AIRLINES - MAY
1929 - 1945
NEW ENGLAND
• MERGED INTO NORTHEAST AIRLINES IN 1945

NATM/P

© PHILIP R. MARTIN 1995 ALL RIGHTS RESERVED. NO REPRODUCTION IN ANY FORM.

McCLAIN AIRLINES - MCL
1983 - 1987
SOUTHWEST US REGIONAL CARRIER
• SUSPENDED OPERATIONS IN 1987

MCL-10B
BRITE GOLDTONE WITH
GOLD & BLACK LOGO

MCL-10W
76MM BRITE GOLDTONE WITH
GOLD & BLACK LOGO

THIS LOGO IS SUPPOSED TO BE "THE PHOENIX", A MYTHICAL BIRD WHO
AROSE FROM THE ASHES - WAS RESURRECTED

McCULLOCH AIRLINES - MCU
1969 - 1975
OPERATED AS A SHUTTLE CARRIER
• OWNER BROUGHT THE "LONDON BRIDGE" TO LAKE HAVASU, AZ IN 1968
• FLEW TOURISTS IN TO SEE BASED FROM LONG BEACH, CA
• TURNED OPERATIONS OVER TO MERCER AIRLINES IN 1975

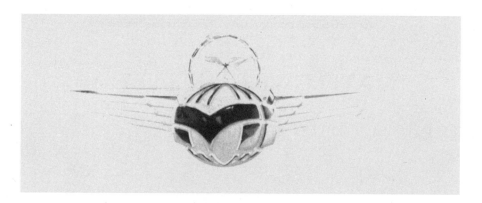

MCU-15W
79MM BRITE GOLDTONE

© PHILIP R. MARTIN 1995 ALL RIGHTS RESERVED. NO REPRODUCTION IN ANY FORM.

MERCER AIRLINES - MER
1972 - 1977
OPERATED AS A PART 135 CHARTER CARRIER
- USED DC-4'S AND DC-6'S TOOK OVER McCUULOGH OPERATION INTO LAKE HAVASU, AZ
- CEASED OPERATIONS AFTER LAST AIRCRAFT CRASHED IN 1977

MER-15W
80MM BRITE/SATIN GOLDTONE WITH A RED "M" IN WHITE CIRCLE

MESA AIRLINES - MSE
1980 - PRESENT
WESTERN US-ROCKY MTS
- STARTED AS MESA AIR SHUTTLE
- CHANGED NAME TO MESA AIRLINES IN 1987
- BEGAN SKYWAY AIRLINES IN 1989
- ACQUIRED ASPEN AIRWAYS ROUTES IN 1990
- ACQUIRED AIR MIDWEST IN 1991 • ACQUIRED WEST AIR IN 1992

MSE-10W
63MM SATIN GOLDTONE WITH BLACK LOGO IN CENTER

© PHILIP R. MARTIN 1995 ALL RIGHTS RESERVED. NO REPRODUCTION IN ANY FORM.

MESABA AVIATION - MES
1966 - PRESENT
NORTH & NORTHWEST US
- CHANGED NAME TO MESABA AIRLINES IN 1973
- NORTHWEST AIRLINK COMMUTER

MES-10W
76MM SILVERTONE, WHITE CENTER

MES-20W
76MM SILVERTONE, RED CENTER

METRO AIRLINES (METRO FLIGHT INC.) - NTR
1965 - PRESENT
MID-WEST US
- ORIGINALLY FORMED AS NASA COMMUTER AIRLINES TO SHUTTLE (PUN !) AEROSPACE PEOPLE FROM HOUSTON TO CAPE CANAVERAL
- NOW OPERATES AS AN AMERICAN EAGLE COMMUTER

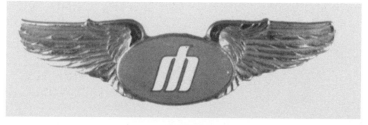

NTR-10B
BRITE GOLDTONE WITH
WHITE SYMBOL IN BLUE CENTER

NTR-10W
76MM BRITE GOLDTONE WITH
WHITE SYMBOL IN BLUE CENTER

© PHILIP R. MARTIN 1995 ALL RIGHTS RESERVED. NO REPRODUCTION IN ANY FORM.

NTR-12W
76MM BRITE GOLDTONE WITH
WHITE SYMBOL IN BLUE CENTER

NTR-15W
76MM BRITE GOLDTONE WITH
WHITE SYMBOL IN BLUE CENTER

METRO NORTHEAST - MNE
1988 - 1991
NORTHEAST US COMMUTER
- BEGAN AS AIR NORTH
- BECAME METRO NORTHEAST AFTER MERGER OF BROCKWAY AIR (NY) AND (VT) IN 1990
- OPERATED AS TRANS WORLD EXPRESS

NATM/P

MGM GRAND AIR - MGM
1987 - PRESENT
INTERNATIONAL - US - AND CHARTER
- LUXURY PASSENGER SERVICE

MGM-10W
76MM BLACK CLOTH WITH GOLD BULLION

MGM-10B
BLACK CLOTH WITH GOLD
BULLION

© PHILIP R. MARTIN 1995 ALL RIGHTS RESERVED. NO REPRODUCTION IN ANY FORM.

MGM-20B
BRITE GOLDTONE WITH
BLUE LION LOGO IN CENTER

MGM-20W
80MM BRITE GOLDTONE WITH
BLUE LION LOGO IN CENTER

MGM-25W
80MM BRITE GOLDTONE WITH BLUE LOGO IN CENTER

MID-CONTINENT AIRLINES - MID
1938 -1952
CENTRAL US
• EVOLVED FROM HANSON TRI-STATE AIR LINES IN 1936
• WAS ALSO KNOWN AS MID-CONTINENT AIR EXPRESS
• MERGED INTO BRANIFF AIRLINES IN 1952

MID-10W
83MM SATIN SILVERTONE WITH BLACK LETTERS

© PHILIP R. MARTIN 1995 ALL RIGHTS RESERVED. NO REPRODUCTION IN ANY FORM.

MID-22W S.D.A.M.
69MM SATIN GOLDTONE WITH ENAMELD BLUE LETTERS & SHEILD

MID-25W
69MM SATIN GOLDTONE WITH ENAMELD BLUE LETTERS & SHEILD

MIDLAND AIR EXPRESS - MDL
1931 - 1932
MID US
• MERGED INTO BRANIFF AIRLINES IN 1932

NATM/P

MID-PACIFIC AIRLINES - MPA
1979 - 1988
PACIFIC-HAWAIIAN ISLANDS COMMUTER
• CEASED OPERATIONS 1988

Mid Pacific Air

MPA-10W
77MM BRITE GOLDTONE

© PHILIP R. MARTIN 1995 ALL RIGHTS RESERVED. NO REPRODUCTION IN ANY FORM.

MIDSTATE AIRLINES - MIS
1964 - PRESENT
MIDWEST US REGIONAL COMMUTER

MIS-10W
82MM BRITE / SATIN SILVERTONE
WITH ORANGE LOGO ON BLUE DISC

MIS-20W
79MM BRITE / SATIN SILVERTONE
WITH ORANGE LOGO ON BLUE DISC

MISSISSIPPI VALLEY AIRLINES - MVA
1969 - 1986
CENTRAL US - MISSISSIPPI VALLEY AREA
• MERGED INTO AIR WISCONSIN IN 1986

MVA-10B
82MM BRITE / SATIN SILVERTONE
WITH ORANGE LOGO ON BLUE DISC

MVA-10W
79MM BRITE / SATIN SILVERTONE
WITH ORANGE LOGO ON BLUE DISC

© PHILIP R. MARTIN 1995 ALL RIGHTS RESERVED. NO REPRODUCTION IN ANY FORM.

MIDWAY AIRLINES - MDW
1976 - 1991
MID-WEST US

- BANKRUPT IN 1991
- TRYING A COMEBACK IN 1995

MDW-10W
95MM SATIN SILVERTONE WITH BLACK OUTLINE LOGO

MDW-20W
86MM BRITE GOLDTONE

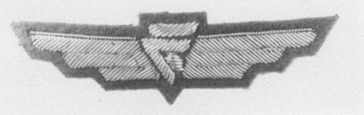

MDW-25W　　　　　　　**MDW-30W**
86MM BRITE GOLDTONE　　98MM BEIGE CLOTH, GOLD BULLION

MDW-35W
98MM BEIGE CLOTH WITH GOLD BULLION

© PHILIP R. MARTIN 1995 ALL RIGHTS RESERVED. NO REPRODUCTION IN ANY FORM.

MIDWAY CONNECTION - MWC
1986 - 1991
MIDWAY AIRLINES COMMUTER SYSTEM
CONSISTING OF :
• FISCHER BROTHERS AVIATION, ILLINOIS FROM 1987
• IOWA AIRWAYS, IOWA FROM 1986

B. Shuey

MWC-12W
78MM SATIN / BRITE GOLDTONE

MID-WEST AIRLINES - MDX
1949 -1952
MID WEST US
• FOUNDED AS IOWA AIRPLANE CO. IN 1933
• CHANGED NAME AND STARTED SERVICE IN 1949
• ENDED OPERATIONS IN 1952

NATM/P

MIDWEST EXPRESS - MWX
1984 - PRESENT
MID-WEST US REGIONAL
• OWNED BY KIMBERLY-CLARK PAPER CO.
• KNOWN AS "THE BEST CARE IN THE AIR"

MWX-10W
86MM BRITE / SATIN SILVERTONE WITH BLACK "ME" IN CENTER

© PHILIP R. MARTIN 1995 ALL RIGHTS RESERVED. NO REPRODUCTION IN ANY FORM.

MWX-20B
BLACK CLOTH WITH SILVER
THREAD "ME" IN CENTER

MWX-20W
82MM BRITE / SATIN SILVERTONE
WITH BLACK "ME" IN CENTER

MOBIL OIL COMPANY - MOB
19 XX - PRESENT
INTERNATIONAL OIL COMPANY

MOB-10B
SATIN GOLDTONE

MOB-10W
81MM SATIN GOLDTONE WITH RED
PEGASUS LOGO IN CENTER

MODERN AIR TRANSPORT - MOD
1946 - 1972
AIR CARGO CARRIER
• MOVED OPERATIONS TO GERMANY • NOW OUT OF BUSINESS

NATM/P

© PHILIP R. MARTIN 1995 ALL RIGHTS RESERVED. NO REPRODUCTION IN ANY FORM.

MOHAWK AIRLINES - MHK
1945 - 1972
EASTERN US
• BEGAN AS ROBINSON AIRLINES IN 1945
• CHANGED NAME TO MOHAWK AIRLINES IN 1952
• MERGED INTO ALLEGHENY AIRLINES IN 1972

L. Ginsburg

MHK-10W
88MM BLACK CLOTH WITH
SILVER BULLION THREAD

K. Taylor

MHK-20B
NATM • BLACK CLOTH WITH
SILVER BULLION THREAD

MHK-20W
NATM • BLACK CLOTH WITH SILVER BULLION THREAD

Koran

MHK-30W
NATM • BLACK CLOTH WITH SILVER BULLION THREAD

© PHILIP R. MARTIN 1995 ALL RIGHTS RESERVED. NO REPRODUCTION IN ANY FORM.

MONARCH AIRLINES - MNA
1945-1950
ROCKY MOUNTAIN AREA - US
• BOUGHT OUT CHALLENGER AIRLINES IN 1949 • MERGED INTO FRONTIER AIRLINES IN 1950

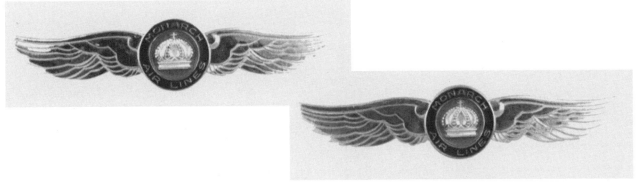

MNA-10W
76MM BRITE GOLDTONE

MNA-20W
76MM BRITE SILVERTONE

MORRIS AIRLINES - MOR
1992 - 1995
US SCHEDULED & CHARTER CARRIER
• FAA CERTIFICATION IN 1992
• BOUGHT OUT BY SOUTHWEST AIRLINES IN 1995

MOR-10W
74MM BRITE GOLDTONE

MOR-20B
74MM BRITE GOLDTONE, BLUE CENTER

MOR-20W
74MM BRITE GOLDTONE WITH BLUE CENTER

© PHILIP R. MARTIN 1995 ALL RIGHTS RESERVED. NO REPRODUCTION IN ANY FORM.

MUSE AIR - MUS
1980-1985
SOUTHWEST & WESTERN US
- CHANGED NAME IN 1985
- PURCHASED BY SOUTHWEST AIRLINES IN 1985

MUS-10B
COPPERTONE

MUS-10W
84MM COPPERTONE

MUS-12W
84MM COPPERTONE

IF A CHECK CAPTAIN'S WING WITH STAR AND WREATH EXISTS,
IT WOULD BE A - **MUS-15W**

© PHILIP R. MARTIN 1995 ALL RIGHTS RESERVED. NO REPRODUCTION IN ANY FORM.

N

NAPLES AIRLINES - NPL
1949 - 1980
EASTCOAST US COMMUTER
• CHANGED NAME TO PROVINCETOWN-BOSTON AIRLINES IN 1980

NATM/P

NATIONAL AIRLINES - NAT
1934 - 1981
US - INTERNATIONAL
• BEGAN AS NATIONAL AIRLINES SYSTEM IN 1934
• INCORPORATED AND CHANGED NAME IN 1937
• MERGED INTO PAN AMERICAN IN 1981

NAT-20W
91MM SATIN SILVERTONE, RED CENTER, SILVER "FLAGPOLE" LOGO
19XX - 1961

Walton

NAT-21W
NATM • BLACK CLOTH, SILVERTHREAD,
RED CENTER GOLD "FLAGPOLE" LOGO
1961 - 1963

NAT-30W
91MM SATIN SILVERTONE, RED CENTER
GOLD "FLAGPOLE" LOGO
1961 - 1963

© PHILIP R. MARTIN 1995 ALL RIGHTS RESERVED. NO REPRODUCTION IN ANY FORM.

NAT-40B
BRITE GOLDTONE WITH
RED & BLUE SYMBOL
<u>1963 - 1968</u>

NAT-40W
90MM SATIN GOLDTONE WITH
RED & BLUE SYMBOL
<u>1963 - 1968</u>

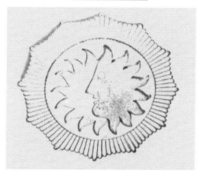

NAT-50B
SATIN GOLDTONE WITH
BRITE SUNBURST FIGURES
<u>1968 - 1981</u>

NAT-50W
91MM SATIN GOLDTONE WITH
BRITE SUNBURST FIGURES
<u>1968 - 1981</u>

NAT-55W
91MM SATIN GOLDTONE WITH BRITE SUNBURST FIGURES
<u>1968 - 1981</u>

NATIONAL AIR TRANSPORT - NTT
1926 - 1930
EASTERN US
• MERGED INTO UNITED AIRLINES IN 1930

NATM/P

© PHILIP R. MARTIN 1995 ALL RIGHTS RESERVED. NO REPRODUCTION IN ANY FORM.

NATIONAL AIRWAYS - NAW
1934
EASTERN US
• BOUGHT BY BOSTON-MAINE AIRWAYS IN 1934

NATM/P

NATIONAL PARKS AIRWAYS - NPW
1931 - 1937
WESTERN US
• CHANGED NAME TO ALFRED FRANK IN 1934 • BOUGHT BY WESTERN AIR EXPRESS IN 1937

K. Taylor

NPW-10W
91MM GOLDTONE WITH GREEN CENTER, YELLOW LETTERS

NATIONAL SKYWAY FREIGHT CORP. - NSF
1945 - 1947
INTERNATIONAL AIR CARGO
• CHANGED NAME TO THE FLYING TIGER LINE INB 1947

Koran

NSF -10W
NATM • BLACK CLOTH WITH SILVER BULLION THREAD,
BLUE ENAMEL CENTER WITH GOLD LINES AND LETTERING

© PHILIP R. MARTIN 1995 ALL RIGHTS RESERVED. NO REPRODUCTION IN ANY FORM.

NEW YORK AIR - NYO
1980 - 1988
EASTERN US COMMUTER SHUTTLE
• CEASED OPERATIONS IN 1988

NYO -10B
FLAT SILVERTONE

NYO -10W
91MM FLAT SILVERTONE

NEW YORK AIRWAYS - NYW
1930 - 1931
EASTERN US
• MERGED INTO EASTERN AIRLINES IN 1931

NATM/P

NEW YORK AIRWAYS - NYA
1951 - 1970
NEW YORK
• HELICOPTERS/ OUT OF BUSINESS IN 1970

NYA-10W
91MM SATIN SILVERTONE

© PHILIP R. MARTIN 1995 ALL RIGHTS RESERVED. NO REPRODUCTION IN ANY FORM.

NEW YORK, PHILA. & WASH. AIRWAY - NYP
1930 - 1933
EASTERN US
• MERGED INTO EASTERN AIRLINES IN 1933

NATM/P

NEW YORK, RIO & BUENOS ARIES AIR LINE - NYR
1929 - 1930
FLORIDA-SO. AMERICA
• MERGED INTO PAN AMERICAN IN 1930

NATM/P

NORTH AMERICAN AIRLINES - NAA
1950 - 1957
INTERNATIONAL
• QUIT IN 1957

Koran

NAA - 10W
NATM/P GOLDTONE
SAME PATTERN AS **TAA-10W**

NORTH CENTRAL AIRLINES - NCA
1947 - 1980
CENTRAL - US
• STARTED AS WISCONSIN CENTRAL AIRLINES
• CHANGED NAME TO NORTH CENTRAL IN 1952
• MERGED WITH SOUTHERN AIRLINES TO FORM REPUBLIC AIRLINES IN 1980

NCA-10W
82MM STERLING WITH RED LOGO
BLUE CIRCLE & WHITE CENTER

NCA-20W
87MM SATIN SILVERTONE WITH
BLUE BIRD FIGURE

© PHILIP R. MARTIN 1995 ALL RIGHTS RESERVED. NO REPRODUCTION IN ANY FORM.

NCA-25W
87MM SATIN SILVERTONE WITH BLUE BIRD FIGURE

NORTHEAST AIRLINES - NEA
1940 - 1971
US
- BEGAN AS BOSTON-MAINE AIRWAYS
- PURCHASED NATIONAL AIRWAYS IN 1937
- CHANGED NAME TO NORTHEAST AIRLINES IN 1940
- MERGED WITH DELTA AIRLINES IN 1971

NEA-10B
GOLDTONE STERLING &
RED CIRCLE WITH A BLUE CENTER

NEA-10W
81MM GOLDTONE STERLING & RED
CIRCLE WITH A BLUE CENTER

NEA-20B
NATM•GOLDTONE, RED LETTERS

NEA-20W
NATM•GOLDTONE, RED LETTERS

© PHILIP R. MARTIN 1995 ALL RIGHTS RESERVED. NO REPRODUCTION IN ANY FORM.

NEA-30B
GOLDTONE WITH RED & BLUE "PILGRIM"

NEA-30W
84 MM GOLDTONE WITH RED & BLUE "PILGRIM"

NEA-32W
84 MM GOLDTONE WITH RED & BLUE "PILGRIM"

NEA-42W
83MM 2 PIECE GOLDTONE

NEA-45W
83MM 2 PIECE GOLDTONE

© PHILIP R. MARTIN 1995 ALL RIGHTS RESERVED. NO REPRODUCTION IN ANY FORM.

NORTHEASTERN INTERNATIONAL AIRWAYS - NEI
1980 - 1987
NORTHEAST US AND FLORIDA
- OUT OF BUSINESS IN 1987

NEI-10W
78MM BRITE GOLDTONE WITH GREEN LETTERING ON A WHITE DISC

NORTHERN AIR LINES - NRT
1928 - 1929
US
- MERGED INTO UNIVERSAL AIR LINES IN 1929

NATM/P

NORTHERN AIR TRANSPORT - NOT
1930 - 1936
ALASKA
- MERGED INTO WIEN ALASKA AIRLINES IN 1936

NATM/P

NORTHERN AIRWAYS - CHP
1967 - PRESENT
NORTHEAST US CHARTER & AIR CARGO
-

NATM/P

© PHILIP R. MARTIN 1995 ALL RIGHTS RESERVED. NO REPRODUCTION IN ANY FORM.

NORTHERN CONSOLIDATED AIRLINES - NCO
1940 - 1968
PACIFIC COAST US - ALASKA
• MERGED INTO WIEN CONSOLIDATED AIRLINES IN 1968

NC0-10W
82MM SATIN GOLDTONE WITH DARK BLUE CENTER

NORTH PACIFIC AIRLINES (NPA) - NPA
1987 - 1990
PACIFIC NORTHWEST - US
• MERGED INTO WEST AIR IN 1990

NPA-10W
82MM BRITE SILVERTONE WITH BLACK CENTER

NORTHWEST (ORIENT) AIRLINES - NWA
1934 - PRESENT
INTERNATIONAL

• BEGAN AS NORTHWEST AIRWAYS IN 1926
• CHANGED NAME TO NORTHWEST AIRLINES IN 1934
• DROPPED "ORIENT" IN THE LATE 1980'S

NWA-10W (see USA-10W)
90MM GOLD WING • IN THE EARLY USE, THE EQUATOR BISECTS "AIR"

© PHILIP R. MARTIN 1995 ALL RIGHTS RESERVED. NO REPRODUCTION IN ANY FORM.

Koran

NWA-20W
NATM • GOLD FILLED, BLUE CENTER FLIGHT ENGINEER WING

NWA-30B
RED, WHITE, BLUE & GOLD

NWA-30W
90MM SATIN GOLDTONE

NORTHWEST AIRWAYS - NWE
1926 - 1934
US
• CHANGED NAME TO NORTHWEST AIRLINES IN 1934

NATM/P

NORTHWEST AIRLINK - NWL
1984 - PRESENT
NORTHWEST US COMMUTER
• EVOLVED FROM SHAWNEE AIRLINES & PRECISION
• CONSISTS OF FOLLOWING REGIONAL AIRLINES :
• BIG SKY AIRLINES, MT FROM 1985 • EXPRESS AIRLINES, TN FROM 1986
• MESABA AIRLINES, MN FROM 1984 • SIMMONS AIRLINES, MN FROM 1986

NWL- 12W
87 MM BRITE / SATIN GOLDTONE, RED LOGO CENTER

© PHILIP R. MARTIN 1995 ALL RIGHTS RESERVED. NO REPRODUCTION IN ANY FORM.

O

ORION AIR - ORN
1980 - 1992
US AIR CARGO

- OUT OF BUSINESS IN 1992

ORN-10W
76MM SATIN GOLDTONE WITH WHITE LOGO ON BLACK DISC

OVERSEAS NATIONAL AIRWAYS (ONA) - ONA
1950 - 1978
US-INTERNATIONAL

- OPERATIONS SUSPENDED IN 1963
- RESUMED OPERATIONS IN 1965
- OUT OF BUSINESS IN 1978

ONA-10W
81MM BLACK CLOTH WITH SILVER BULLION WITH GREEN CENTER

ONA-20B
FLAT SILVERTONE

© PHILIP R. MARTIN 1995 ALL RIGHTS RESERVED. NO REPRODUCTION IN ANY FORM.

ONA-20W
80MM FLAT SILVERTONE

ONA-22W
80MM FLAT SILVERTONE

ONA-25W
80MM FLAT SILVERTONE

OXY PETROLEUM - OXY
19XX - PRESENT
TULSA BASED OIL COMPANY
• CORPORATE ENERGY ACTIVITIES

OXY-10W
71MM SATIN GOLDTONE WITH RED LETTERS ON A BLUE & WHITE CENTER

OZARK AIR LINES - OZA
1943 - 1986
US REGIONAL & NATIONAL CARRIER
• MERGED INTO TWA IN 1986

OZA-10B
GOLD FILLED OR SATIN/BRITE GOLDTONE

OZA-12W
81MM GOLD FILLED OR SATIN/BRITE GOLDTONE

OZA-15W
81MM GOLD FILLED OR SATIN/BRITE GOLDTONE

© PHILIP R. MARTIN 1995 ALL RIGHTS RESERVED. NO REPRODUCTION IN ANY FORM.

OZA-25W
83MM BRITE GOLDTONE WITH DARK GREEN CENTER & LOGO

OZA-30W
93MM BRITE GOLDTONE

P

PACIFIC AIR LINES - PAC
1946 - 1967
WESTERN US

- STARTED AS SOUTHWEST AIRWAYS IN 1946
- CHANGED NAME TO PACIFIC AIR LINES IN 1958
- MERGED WITH BONANZA AIRLINES AND WEST COAST AIRLINES TO BECOME AIR WEST 1967

PAC-10B   **PAC-10W**
SATIN SILVERTONE   72MM BRITE SILVERTONE,
                             BLUE OVAL & RED LETTERS

PACIFIC AIR TRANSPORT - PAT
1926 - 1927
US
- MERGED INTO BOEING AIR TRANSPORT

NATM/P

PACIFIC ALASKA AIRLINES - PAK
1975 - 1986
ALASKA & CONTINENTAL US

- OUT OF BUSINESS IN 1986

NATM/P

PACIFIC ALASKA AIRWAYS - PAW
1935 - 1941
ALASKA
- MERGED INTO PAN AM IN 1941

NATM/P

© PHILIP R. MARTIN 1995 ALL RIGHTS RESERVED. NO REPRODUCTION IN ANY FORM.

PACIFIC EAST AIR - PEA
1982 - 1984
CALIFORNIA - HAWAIIAN CHARTER
• OUT OF BUSINESS IN 1984

PEA-10W
81MM FLAT SILVERTONE

PACIFIC EXPRESS - PAX
1981 - 1984
WESTERN US COMMUTER
• OUT OF BUSINESS IN 1984

PAX-10W
82MM FLAT SILVERTONE

PACIFIC MARINE AIRWAYS - PMA
1922 - 1928
SOUTHERN CALIFORNIA - AVALON
• MERGED INTO WESTERN AIR EXPRESS IN 1928

NATM/P

PACIFIC NORTHERN AIRLINES - PNO
1945 - 1967
WESTERN US - ALASKA
- FOUNDED AS WOODLEY AIRWAYS IN 1945
- CHANGED NAME TO PACIFIC NORTHERN 1947
- MERGED INTO WESTERN AIRLINES IN 1967

PNO-10B
STERLING WITH BLUE ALASKAN FLAG ON A RED CENTER, 3 STREAKS

PNO-10W
76MM STERLING WITH BLUE
ALASKAN FLAG ON A RED CENTER

PNO-20W
82MM STERLING WITH BLUE
ALASKAN FLAG ON A RED CENTER

PACIFIC SEABOARD AIRLINES - PSE
1933 - 1934
SAN FRAN.-L.A. & MISSISSIPPI VALEY MAIL ROUTE
- CHANGED NAME TO CHICAGO SOUTHERN IN 1934

NATM/P

© PHILIP R. MARTIN 1995 ALL RIGHTS RESERVED. NO REPRODUCTION IN ANY FORM.

PACIFIC SOUTHWEST AIRLINES (PSA) - PSA
1945 - 1986
WESTERN US

• MERGED INTO US AIR IN 1986

PSA-22W
85MM BLACK CLOTH WITH
SILVER BULLION
<u>1970 - 1986</u>

PSA-25W
85MM BLACK CLOTH WITH
SILVER BULLION
<u>1970 - 1986</u>

PSA-30B
STERLING OR 1/20 GOLD
<u>1970 - 1986</u>

PSA-30W
82MM STERLING OR 1/20 GOLD
<u>1970 - 1986</u>

PSA-32W
82MM STERLING OR 1/20 GOLD
<u>1970 - 1986</u>

PSA-35W
82MM STERLING OR 1/20 GOLD
<u>1970 - 1986</u>

© PHILIP R. MARTIN 1995 ALL RIGHTS RESERVED. NO REPRODUCTION IN ANY FORM.

PSA-40W
80MM BLUE CLOTH WITH WHITE THREAD
1970 - 1986

PSA-42W
80MM BLUE CLOTH WITH WHITE THREAD
1970 - 1986

PSA-45W
80MM BLUE CLOTH WITH WHITE THREAD
1970 - 1986

© PHILIP R. MARTIN 1995 ALL RIGHTS RESERVED. NO REPRODUCTION IN ANY FORM.

PAN AMERICAN AFRICA - PAR
1941 - 1945
AFRICA
- FORMED TO FLY SUPPLIES AND MATERIAL TO AFRICA DURING WW2
- PHASED OUT AT THE END OF THE WAR

Koran
PAR-10W
NATM • GOLD OR GOLDTONE

PAN AMERICAN FERRIES - PAF
1941 - 1945
INTERNATIONAL
- FORMED TO FLY LEND LEASE AIRCRAFT TO THE ALLIES DURING WW2
- PHASED OUT SHORTLY AFTER THE END OF THE WAR

Koran
PAF-10W
NATM • GOLD OR GOLDTONE

© PHILIP R. MARTIN 1995 ALL RIGHTS RESERVED. NO REPRODUCTION IN ANY FORM.

PAN AMERICAN-GRACE AIRWAYS (PANAGRA) - PGR
1929 - 1967
SOUTH AMERICA
• MERGED WITH BRANIFF AIRLINES IN 1967

NATM/P

PAN AMERICAN WORLD AIRWAYS - PAA
1927 - 1991
INTERNATIONAL CARRIER

• BANKRUPT IN 1991

S.D.A.M.

PAA-10W
TYPE ONE   92MM STERLING WITH BLUE OVAL & BLUE WINGED LOGO
1928 - 1930

TYPE TWO IS 10K GOLD or GOLD FILLED WITH DEEP BLUE ENAMELING. THE OVERHEAD VIEW IS OVER SOUTH AMERICA WITH SOME OF NORTH AMERICA. THE BLUE IS SOLID. USED FROM **1930 -1944**

PAA-20B
SATIN GOLD OR GF -TYPE TWO
1930 -1944

PAA-20W
57MM SATIN GOLD OR GF -TYPE TWO
BLUE RECTANGLE WITH ONE STAR-
JUNIOR PILOT - 1930 -1944

© PHILIP R. MARTIN 1995 ALL RIGHTS RESERVED. NO REPRODUCTION IN ANY FORM.

PAA-22W
57MM SATIN GOLD OR GOLDPLATED
- TYPE TWO - BLUE RECTANGLE
WITH TWO STARS- SENIOR PILOT
<u>1930 -1944</u>

PAA-25W
57MM SATIN GOLD OR GOLDPLATED
- TYPE TWO - BLUE RECTANGLE
WITH THREE STARS-MASTER PILOT
<u>1930 - 1944</u>

<u>**TYPE THREE**</u> IS EITHER 10K GOLD or GOLD FILLED WITH BLUE ENAMELING. THE VIEW OF THE GLOBE OVER THE BLUE NORTH ATLANTIC OCEAN. LATITUDE AND LONGITUDE LINES ARE USED.
<u>1945 - 1959</u>

PAA-30B
10K GOLD OR GOLDPLATED
-TYPE THREE -   <u>1945 - 1959</u>

PAA-30W
57MM 10K GOLD OR GOLDPLATED
-TYPE THREE - BLUE RECTANGLE
WITH ONE STAR - JUNIOR PILOT
<u>1945 - 1959</u>

© PHILIP R. MARTIN 1995 ALL RIGHTS RESERVED. NO REPRODUCTION IN ANY FORM.

PAA-32W
57MM 10K GOLD OR GOLDPLATED -TYPE THREE - BLUE RECTANGLE
WITH TWO STARS - SENIOR PILOT 1945 - 1959

PAA-35W
57MM 10K GOLD OR GOLDPLATED -TYPE THREE - BLUE RECTANGLE
WITH THREE STARS - MASTER PILOT 1945 - 1959

TYPE FOUR IS 10K GOLD or GOLD FILLED WITH BLUE ENAMELING. THE GLOBE LOGO WITH RAISED AND CURVED LATITUDE LINES AND RAISED "PAN AM".   USED FROM **1959 - 1979**

PAA-40B
GOLD GLOBE LOGO IN CENTER
-TYPE FOUR

PAA-40W
57MM 10K GOLD OR GOLD FILLED
-TYPE FOUR - BLUE RECTANGLE
**WITH ONE STAR - FIRST OFFICER
ALSO USED FOR FLIGHT ENGINEER
1959 - 1979**

© PHILIP R. MARTIN 1995 ALL RIGHTS RESERVED. NO REPRODUCTION IN ANY FORM.

PAA-41W
57MM 10K GOLD OR GOLD FILLED
-TYPE FOUR -BLUE RECTANGLE WITH
TWO STARS - JUNIOR CAPTAIN
<u>1959 - 1979</u>

PAA-42W
57MM 10K GOLD OR GOLD FILLED
-TYPE FOUR -BLUE RECTANGLE
WITH THREE STARS & STAR ABOVE GLOBE-
SENIOR CAPTAIN   <u>1959 - 1979</u>

Koran

PAA-43W
57MM SATIN/BRITE 10K GOLD OR
GOLDTONE BLUE RECTANGLE WITH
THREE STARS - JUNIOR CAPTAIN
<u>1959 -1979</u>

PAA-45W
57MM SATIN/BRITE 10K GOLD OR
GOLDTONE BLUE RECTANGLE WITH
THREE STARS AND STAR & WREATH
ABOVE CENTER - CHECK CAPTAIN
(CHECK AIRMAN) <u>1959 -1979</u>

© PHILIP R. MARTIN 1995 ALL RIGHTS RESERVED. NO REPRODUCTION IN ANY FORM.

TYPE FIVE IS GOLD FILLED OR GOLDTONE WITH BLUE ENAMELING. THE GLOBE LOGO WITH RAISED AND CURVED LATITUDE LINES AND RAISED "PAN AM". USED **1979 - 1991**

PAA-50B
BRIGHT GOLDTONE - **TYPE FIVE - 1980 -1991**

PAA-50W
72MM SATIN/BRITE GOLDTONE -TYPE FIVE - BLUE RECTANGLE
WITH ONE STAR - FLIGHT ENGINEER   1980 - 1991

PAA-51W
72MM SATIN/BRITE GOLDTONE - TYPE FIVE - BLUE RECTANGLE
WITH ONE STAR AND WREATH ABOVE CENTER - CHECK FLIGHT ENGINEER
Known as "the toilet seat" on the Flight Deck
1980 - 1991

© PHILIP R. MARTIN 1995 ALL RIGHTS RESERVED. NO REPRODUCTION IN ANY FORM.

PAA-52W
72MM SATIN/BRITE GOLDTONE - TYPE FIVE - BLUE RECTANGLE
WITH THREE STARS - JUNIOR CAPTAIN
1980 - 1991

PAA-53W
72MM SATIN/BRITE GOLDTONE - TYPE FIVE - BLUE RECTANGLE
WITH THREE STARS AND A STAR ABOVE CENTER - SENIOR CAPTAIN
1980-1991

PAA-55W
72MM SATIN/BRITE GOLDTONE - TYPE FIVE- RECTANGLE
WITH THREE STARS AND STAR AND WREATH ABOVE CENTER GLOBE
CHECK CAPTAIN or CHECK AIRMAN
1980-1991

© PHILIP R. MARTIN 1995 ALL RIGHTS RESERVED. NO REPRODUCTION IN ANY FORM.

PAN AM EXPRESS - PXX
1988 - 1991
EASTERN REGIONAL CARRIER-US
- STARTED AS RANSOME AIRLINES • BECAME PAN AM EXPRESS IN 1988
- CHANGED INTO CURRENT OPERATION AS TWA EXPRESS IN 1991

TYPE FIVE WING WITH
PAN AM EXPRESS" ON LOGO

PXX-10B
GOLDTONE

PXX-10W
NATM/P • GOLDTONE

PAN AM GMRD (GUIDED MISSLE RANGE DIVISION) - PGM
19 XX - 19 XX
- DIVISION OF PAN AM WHICH MAINTAINED FLORIDA GUIDED MISSLE RANGE

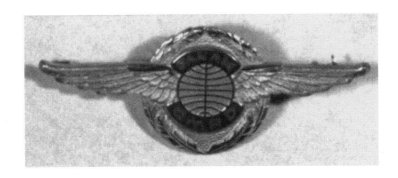

PGM-10W
57MM SATIN GOLDTONE

© PHILIP R. MARTIN 1995 ALL RIGHTS RESERVED. NO REPRODUCTION IN ANY FORM.

PARADISE ISLAND AIRLINES - PDX
19 XX - 19 XX
EAST COAST TOURIST COMMUTER
• OWNED BY MERV GRIFFIN TO FLY TOURISTS INTO HIS CARRIBEAN RESORT

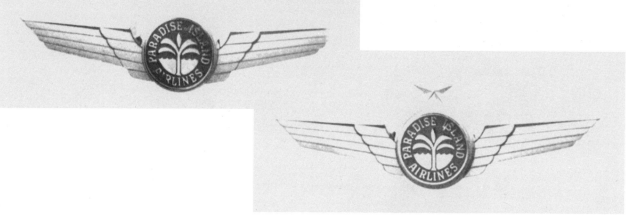

PDX-10W
81MM SATIN GOLDTONE, GREEN CENTER

PDX-12W
81MM SATIN GOLDTONE, GREEN CENTER

PBA - SEE PROVINCETOWN-BOSTON AIRLINE

PEN AIR - SEE PENNINSULA AIRWAYS

PENNINSULA AIRWAYS - PEN
1955 - PRESENT
SOUTHWEST ALASKA REGIONAL COMMUTER
• INCORPORATED IN 1965 • CHANGED NAME TO "PEN AIR" IN 1992

PEN-10W
77MM BRITE SILVERTONE WITH BLACK LETTERS

PEN-20W
77MM BRITE SILVERTONE WITH RED LETTERS

© PHILIP R. MARTIN 1995 ALL RIGHTS RESERVED. NO REPRODUCTION IN ANY FORM.

PENNSYLVANIA AIR LINES - PNA
1931 - 1936
EASTERN US
• OPERATED MAIL ROUTE FROM 1927 • MERGED INTO PENN-CENTRAL AIRLINES IN 1936

K. Taylor

PNA-10B
GOLDTONE WITH RED "P"

K. Taylor

PNA-10W
72 MM GOLDTONE WITH RED "P"

PENNSYLVANIA AIRLINES - PNC
1965 - PRESENT
REGIONAL COMMUTER

• BEGAN SERVICE AS PENNSYLVANIA COMMUTER AIRLINE UNTIL 1980
• OPERATES AS A US AIR EXPRESS OPERATOR

NATM/P

PENNSYLVANIA-CENTRAL AIRLINES - PCA
1936 - 1948
EASTERN US REGIONAL
• RENAMED CAPITAL AIRLINES IN 1948

PCA-10B
GOLD FILLED OVER STERLING
RED AND BLUE ENAMELED CENTER

PCA-10W
91MM GOLD FILLED OVER STERLING

© PHILIP R. MARTIN 1995 ALL RIGHTS RESERVED. NO REPRODUCTION IN ANY FORM.

PCA-20W
91MM GOLD FILLED OVER STERLING

PEOPLEXPRESS AIRLINES - PEO
1980 - 1989
US SCHEDULED OPERATIONS
• MERGED WITH FRONTIER AIRLINES IN 1986
• CEASED OPERATIONS IN 1989

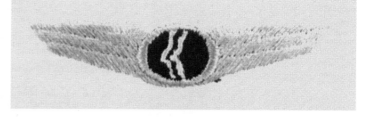

PEO-10W
83MM SATIN/BRITE GOLDTONE
WITH LOGO ON MAROON CENTER

PEO-20W
83MM WHITE CLOTH WITH MAROON
THREAD AND YELLOW HIGHLIGHTS

PHH AIR - RYN
1987 - PRESENT
AIR CARGO & CHARTER OPERATIONS
• CHANGED NAME FROM RYAN INTERNATIONAL AIRLINES IN 1987

NATM/P

© PHILIP R. MARTIN 1995 ALL RIGHTS RESERVED. NO REPRODUCTION IN ANY FORM.

PHILLIPS PETROLEUM CO. "66" - PIL
1934 - PRESENT
OIL COMPANY

PIL-15W
74MM SATIN SILVERTONE

PIEDMONT AIRLINES - PAI
1948 - 1989
EASTERN US

- PURCHASED EMPIRE AIRLINES IN 1989
- MERGED INTO US AIR IN 1989

PAI-10W
82MM STERLING WITH RED, BLUE & WHITE LOGO ON LIGHT BLUE CIRCLE
<u>1948 -1962</u>

PAI-12W
82MM STERLING WITH RED, BLUE & WHITE LOGO ON LIGHT BLUE CIRCLE
<u>1948 -1962</u>

© PHILIP R. MARTIN 1995 ALL RIGHTS RESERVED. NO REPRODUCTION IN ANY FORM.

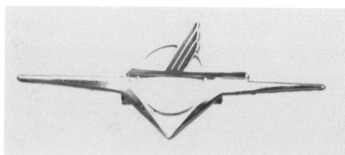

PAI-20W
61MM SILVERTONE, MAROON LOGO
1962 -1974

PAI-22W L. Ginsburg
61MM SILVERTONE, MAROON LOGO
1962 -1974

PAI-30W
75MM BLACK CLOTH WITH SILVER
AND LOGO ON STERLING DISC
1974 -1989

PAI-32W
75MM BLACK CLOTH WITH SILVER
AND LOGO ON STERLING DISC
1974 -1989

PILGRIM AIRLINES - PLG
1962 - 1987
EAST COAST US AND CANADA
• OUT OF BUSINESS IN 1987

NATM/P

© PHILIP R. MARTIN 1995 ALL RIGHTS RESERVED. NO REPRODUCTION IN ANY FORM.

PINEHURST AIRLINES - PIN
1973 -1981
EAST COAST CHARTER & COMMUTER SERVICE
• OUT OF BUSINESS IN 1981

Koran

PIN-15W
NATM • SILVERTONE

PIONEER AIR LINES - PER
1945 - 1955
WESTERN US
• FOUNDED AS ESSAIR IN 1939 • RENAMED PIONEER AIR LINES IN 1943
• STARTED PASSENGER SERVICE IN 1945
• MERGED WITH CONTINENTAL AIRLINES IN 1955

PER-10W
NATM • GOLDTONE

© PHILIP R. MARTIN 1995 ALL RIGHTS RESERVED. NO REPRODUCTION IN ANY FORM.

PIONEER AIRLINES - PIO
1976 - 1986
ROCKY MOUNTAIN AREA - US
• OPERATED AS A CONTINENTAL EXPRESS COMMUTER
• OUT OF BUSINESS IN 1986

PIO-20W
NATM • SILVERTONE, RED, WHITE & BLUE ENAMEL CENTER

PITCAIRN AVIATION - PIT
1927 - 1928
EAST US
• MERGED INTO EASTERN AIR TRANSPORT IN 1928

NATM/P

POCONO AIRLINES - POC
1965 - 1990
NORTHEAST US COMMUTER
• BECAME ALLEGHENY COMMUTER IN 1965
• BECAME A US AIR EXPRESS CARRIER IN 1983
• CEASED OPERATIONS IN 1990

POC-10W
NATM • SILVERTONE

© PHILIP R. MARTIN 1995 ALL RIGHTS RESERVED. NO REPRODUCTION IN ANY FORM.

PORTS OF CALL AIRLINES - PRT
1968 - 1989
US & INTERNATIONAL CHARTER
• MERGED INTO AMERICAN TRANS AIR IN 1989

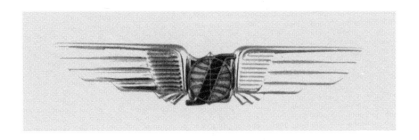

PRT-10W
86MM BRITE SILVERTONE WITH GLOBE CENTER WITH BLUE LOGO

PRECISION (VALLEY) AVIATION - PRE
1977 - PRESENT
NORTHEAST COMMUTER-US
• MERGED WITH WINNIPESAUKEE AIRLINES IN 1980
• OPERATES AS A NORTHWEST AIRLINK

NATM/P

PRESIDENTIAL AIR - PRA
1995 - PRESENT
CHARTER AND REGIONAL CARRIER

PRA-15W
70MM SATIN / BRITE GOLDTONE WITH BLUE CENTER

© PHILIP R. MARTIN 1995 ALL RIGHTS RESERVED. NO REPRODUCTION IN ANY FORM.

PRESIDENTIAL AIRWAYS - PRS
1985 - 1989
MID-ATLANTIC REGIONAL CARRIER
- STARTED AS A CONTINENTAL FEEDER
- BECAME A UNITED EXPRESS CARRIER IN 1988
- OUT OF BUSINESS IN 1989

PRS-10W
70MM SATIN / BRITE GOLDTONE

PRESIDENTIAL EXPRESS - PXP
1965 - 1989
EASTERN US REGIONAL COMMUTER
- ORIGINALLY FOUNDED IN 1965 AS COLGAN AIRWAYS
- OPERATED AS SUBSIDIARY OF PRESIDENTIAL AIRWAYS & UNITED EXPRESS COMMUTER

NATM/P

PRIDE AIR - PRI
1985 - 1986
- STRIKING CONTINENTAL PILOTS ATTEMPTS AT STARTING A RIVAL AIRLINE

PRI-10B **PRI-15W**
FLAT SILVERTONE   80MM FLAT SILVERTONE

© PHILIP R. MARTIN 1995 ALL RIGHTS RESERVED. NO REPRODUCTION IN ANY FORM.

PRINAIR - PRN
1964 - 1985
PUERT RICO- CARRIBEAN AREA
- STARTED BUSINESS AS PONCE AIR
- CHANGED NAME TO PRINAIR IN 1965
- OUT OF BUSINESS IN 1985

PRN-10W
84 MM FLAT SILVERTONE

PROVINCETOWN-BOSTON AIRLINE (PBA) - PBA
1980 - PRESENT
EAST COAST US COMMUTER
- UNTIL 1980 KNOWN AS NAPLES AIRLINES

PBA-10W
80MM SATIN GOLDTONE WITH
WHITE BIRD ON BLUE CENTER

PBA-20W
73MM BLACK CLOTH WITH GOLD
AND SILVER BULLION LOGO

© PHILIP R. MARTIN 1995 ALL RIGHTS RESERVED. NO REPRODUCTION IN ANY FORM.

Q

QUEST AIRLINES - QST
1987 - 1990
WESTERN US REGIONAL COMMUTER
• OUT OF BUSINESS IN 1990

QST-10W
63 MM BRITE GOLDTONE WITH BLUE CENTER

R
RANSOME AIRLINES - RAN
1966 - 1988
EASTERN US REGIONAL COMMUTER
- STARTED AS ALLEGHENY COMMUTER UNTIL 1982
- CHANGED NAME INTO PAN AM EXPRESS IN 1988

RAN-12W
80MM BRITE SILVERTONE WITH "R" LOGO IN BLUE SQUARE

RAPID AIR TRANSPORT - RAP
1929 - 1933
MID-WEST US
- MERGED WITH HANFORD AND LATER BRANIFF AIRLINES

NATM/P

READING AIRLINES - REA
1957 - 1968
EAST AND NOTHEAST US COMMUTER
- CHANGED NAME IN 1968 TO SUBURBAN AIRLINES

NATM/P

© PHILIP R. MARTIN 1995 ALL RIGHTS RESERVED. NO REPRODUCTION IN ANY FORM.

REEVE ALEUTIAN AIRWAYS - RAA
1931 - PRESENT
ALASKA

- STARTED AS REEVE AIRWAYS
- BECAME REEVE ALEUTIAN AIRWAYS IN 1951

Walton

RAA-10W
NATM • BLACK BULLION WITH ALASKA OUTLINE

RAA-40W
80MM FLAT SILVERTONE WITH BLUE & RED LETTERS ON A WHITE CIRCLE

RELIANT AIRLINES - RLT
1984 - PRESENT
MIDWEST US REGIONAL COMMUTER

NATM/P

© PHILIP R. MARTIN 1995 ALL RIGHTS RESERVED. NO REPRODUCTION IN ANY FORM.

RENO AIR - RNO
1992 - PRESENT
WERTERN US REGIONAL CARRIER

B. Shuey

RNO-15W
80MM BRITE GOLDTONE OR SILVERTONE WITH
GREEN MOUNTAINS ON A WHITE CIRCLE

RENOWN AIRLINES - REN
1975 - PRESENT
US
FREIGHT AND CHARTER

REN-10W
76MM BRITE SILVERTONE WITH RED CENTER

© PHILIP R. MARTIN 1995 ALL RIGHTS RESERVED. NO REPRODUCTION IN ANY FORM.

REPUBLIC AIRLINES - REP
1979 - 1986
US NATIONAL CARRIER
- CREATED FROM MERGER OF SOUTHERN AND NORTH CENTRAL AIRLINES
- ABSORBED HUGHES AIR WEST IN 1980
- MERGED WITH NORTHWEST AIRLINES IN 1986

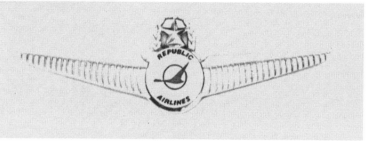

REP-10W
88MM SATIN SILVERTONE WITH
BLUE BIRD LOGO IN CENTER

REP-15W
88MM SATIN SILVERTONE WITH
BLUE BIRD LOGO IN CENTER

RESORT AIR - LOF
1982 - 1990
MIDWEST US REGIONAL COMMUTER
- OPERATED AS A TRANS WORLD EXPRESS COMMUTER

NATM/P

RESORT AIRLINES - RES
1945 -1960
CARRIBEAN CRUISES
- CEASED OPERATIONS IN 1955
- CONTINUED AIR CARGO OPERATIONS UNTIL 1960

NATM/P

© PHILIP R. MARTIN 1995 ALL RIGHTS RESERVED. NO REPRODUCTION IN ANY FORM.

RICH INTERNATIONAL AIRWAYS - RIA
1970 - 1985
US AND INTERNATIONAL PASSENGERS & AIR CARGO
• CEASED OPERATIONS IN 1985

NATM/P

RIDDLE AIRLINES - RDL
1946 - 1963
INTERNATIONAL AIR CARGO
• BECAME AIRLIFT INTERNATIONAL IN 1963

RID-10W
BLACK CLOTH WITH SILVER THREAD AND YELLOW CENTER

RIO AIRWAYS - RIO
1967 - 1987
SOUTHWEST US COMMUTER
• MERGED WITH HOOD AIRLINES IN 1970
• ABSORBED DAVIS AIRLINES IN 1977
• OUT OF BUSINESS IN 1987

RIO-10B　　　　　**RIO-10W**
BRITE GOLDTONE　　75MM BRITE GOLDTONE

© PHILIP R. MARTIN 1995 ALL RIGHTS RESERVED. NO REPRODUCTION IN ANY FORM.

ROBERTSON AIRLINES - RBT
1926 - 1934
MID-US
• SOLD OPERATION TO WEDELL/WILLIS IN 1934

NATM/P

ROBINSON AIRLINES - RBN
1946 - 1953
NORTHEASTERN US
• CHANGED NAME TO MOHAWK AIRLINES IN 1953

NATM/P

ROCKY MOUNTAIN AIRWAYS - RMA
1966 - PRESENT
ROCKY MT. AREA REGIONAL CARRIER
• OPERATES AS A CONTINENTAL EXPRESS COMMUTER

RMA-10W
55MM STERLING

RMA-20W
55MM GOLDTONE

© PHILIP R. MARTIN 1995 ALL RIGHTS RESERVED. NO REPRODUCTION IN ANY FORM.

ROSENBALM AVIATION - RBM
1961 - PRESENT
US CARGO OPERATIONS

RMB-10W
80MM SATIN GOLDTONE WITH ORANGE JET ON BLUE CENTER

ROSS AVIATION - NRG
1953 - PRESENT
SOUTHWEST US - AIR CHARTER

NRG-10W
80MM BRITE / SATIN GOLDTONE

ROYAL AMERICAN AIRWAYS - RAR
1980 - 1987
SOUTHWEST US COMMUTER
• OUT OF BUSINESS IN 1987

Koran

RAR-1OB
BRITE GOLDTONE

Koran

RAR-12W
NATM • BRITE GOLDTONE

© PHILIP R. MARTIN 1995 ALL RIGHTS RESERVED. NO REPRODUCTION IN ANY FORM.

ROYAL HAWAIIAN AIR SERVICE - RHA
1965 - 1966
HAWAIIAN COMMUTER
- BEGAN AS HAWAII WINGS IN 1963
- CHANGED NAME IN 1965

Nichols

RHA-1OW
NATM • GOLDTONE, WHITE LOGO ON BLACK CENTER

ROYAL WEST AIRLINES - RYW
1986 -1988
WESTERN US REGIONAL CARRIER
- BANKRUPT IN 1988

RYW-15W
77MM SATIN / BRITE GOLDTONE

© PHILIP R. MARTIN 1995 ALL RIGHTS RESERVED. NO REPRODUCTION IN ANY FORM.

ROYALE AIR LINES - RAY
1969-1990
SOUTHERN US REGIONAL COMMUTER
- DECLARED BANKRUPTCY IN 1987
- OUT OF BUSINESS IN 1990

RAY-10B
SILVERTONE WITH MAGENTA "FLUER DE LIS" ON WHITE SHEILD

RAY-10W
NATM • SILVERTONE WITH MAGENTA "FLUER DE LIS" ON WHITE SHEILD

RYAN AIRLINES - RYL
1925 - 1927
- CEASED IN 1927

NATM/P

© PHILIP R. MARTIN 1995 ALL RIGHTS RESERVED. NO REPRODUCTION IN ANY FORM.

RYAN AVIATION - RYA
1973 - UNKNOWN
MID-WEST AND EASTERN US

NATM/P

RYAN INTERNATIONAL AIRLINES - RYN
1957 - PRESENT
US CARRIER PRIMARILY AIR CARGO & CHARTER

• RENAMED PHH AIR IN 1987

RYN-10W
75MM BRITE / SATIN SILVERTONE

© PHILIP R. MARTIN 1995 ALL RIGHTS RESERVED. NO REPRODUCTION IN ANY FORM.

S

SABRE AIRLINES - SBR
1978 - 1991
EASTERN US CHARTER & AIR CARGO
• OUT OF BUSINESS IN 1991

SBR-15W
80MM BRITE/SATIN GOLDTONE

ST. PETERSBURG-TAMPA AIRBOAT LINE - STP
1913 - 1914
FLORIDA
• US FIRST OPERATING AIRLINE
• CEASED OPERATING 23 MILE ROUTE

NATM/P

SAN JUAN AIRLINES - SJC
1947 - 1989
PACIFIC NORTHWEST REGIONAL
• OUT OF BUSINESS IN 1989

SJC-10W
76MM BLACK CLOTH WITH GOLD BULLION & SILVER PROPELLER

© PHILIP R. MARTIN 1995 ALL RIGHTS RESERVED. NO REPRODUCTION IN ANY FORM.

SATURN AIRWAYS - SAT
1948 - 1976
INTERNATIONAL AIR CARGO
• ACQUIRED AAXICO AIRLINES IN 1965
• MERGED WITH TRANS-INTERNATIONAL IN 1976

SAT-10B
STERLING OR FLAT SILVERTONE, BLUE "SATURN" PLANET ON A WHITE CIRCLE

SAT-10W
76MM STERLING OR FLAT SILVERTONE, BLUE "SATURN" PLANET ON A WHITE CIRCLE

SAT-12W
76MM STERLING OR FLAT SILVERTONE, BLUE "SATURN" PLANET ON A WHITE CIRCLE

© PHILIP R. MARTIN 1995 ALL RIGHTS RESERVED. NO REPRODUCTION IN ANY FORM.

SCENIC AIRLINES - SCE
1967 - PRESENT
GRAND CANYON SCENIC
LAS VEGAS-SCOTTSDALE

SCE-10W
80MM BRITE GOLDTONE WITH A SMALL RAINBOW IN THE CENTER

SCE-12W
80MM BRITE GOLDTONE WITH A SMALL RAINBOW IN THE CENTER

SCE-15W
80MM BRITE GOLDTONE WITH A SMALL RAINBOW IN THE CENTER

SEAIR - SMO
1941 - 1987
ALASKAN REGIONAL CARRIER
• OUT OF BUSINESS IN 1987

NATM/P

© PHILIP R. MARTIN 1995 ALL RIGHTS RESERVED. NO REPRODUCTION IN ANY FORM.

SEABOARD & WESTERN AIRLINES - SEA
1946 -1980
INTERNATIONAL AIR CARGO
• RENAMED "WORLD" IN 1961
• MERGED WITH FLYING TIGERS IN 1980

SEA-10B
SATIN GOLDTONE WITH SILVER BIRD LOGO IN CENTER & RED "SW"

SEA-10W
82MM SATIN GOLDTONE WITH SILVER BIRD LOGO IN CENTER & RED "SW"

SEA-12W
82MM SATIN GOLDTONE WITH SILVER BIRD LOGO IN CENTER & RED"SW"

© PHILIP R. MARTIN 1995 ALL RIGHTS RESERVED. NO REPRODUCTION IN ANY FORM.

SEDALLIA-MARSHALL- BOONVILLE STAGE LINE (SMB)
- SMB

1930 - 1980
MIDWEST AND SOUTHWEST US REGIONAL CARRIER
• FOUNDED IN 1930 • BEGAN SCHEDULED OPERATIONS IN 1967
• OUT OF BUSINESS IN 1980

Koran

SMB-10W
NATM • GOLDTONE WITH BLACK CENTER & STAGECOACH

SMB-22W
60MM BLACK CLOTH WITH SILVER BULLION

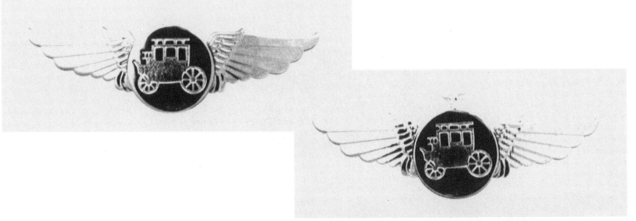

SMB-30W
70MM BRITE SILVERTONE WITH
STAGECOACH LOGO IN CENTER

SMB-32W
70MM BRITE SILVERTONE WITH
STAGECOACH LOGO IN CENTER

© PHILIP R. MARTIN 1995 ALL RIGHTS RESERVED. NO REPRODUCTION IN ANY FORM.

SHAWNEE AIRLINES - SHA
1968 - 1980
GREAT LAKES & MID WEST US COMMUTER / FLORIDA & BAHAMAS
• OUT OF BUSINESS IN 1980

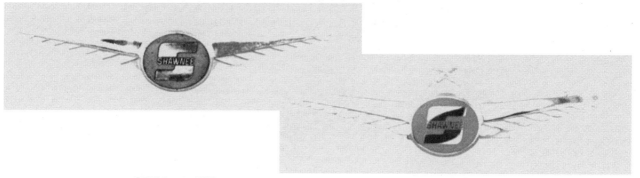

SHA-10W
64MM BRITE/SATIN GOLDTONE
WITH RED/ORANGE CENTER

SHA-15W
64MM BRITE/SATIN GOLDTONE
WITH RED/ORANGE CENTER

SIERRA PACIFIC AIRLINES - SPA
1976 - PRESENT
WESTERN US REGIONAL CARRIER

NATM/P

SIMMONS AIRLINES - SYM
1979 - PRESENT
MID-WEST US COMMUTER
• BECAME AMERICAN EAGLE COMMUTER IN 1988

SYM-10B
BLACK CLOTH WITH SILVERTONE CENTER

© PHILIP R. MARTIN 1995 ALL RIGHTS RESERVED. NO REPRODUCTION IN ANY FORM.

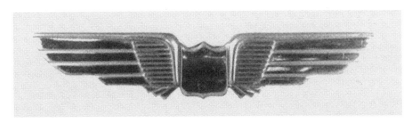

SYM-10W
86MM BRITE GOLDTONE
PLAIN WING - NO LOGO

SYM-12W
86MM BRITE GOLDTONE
PLAIN WING - NO LOGO

THE COMPANY HAS AN IDENTICAL SILVERTONE ISSUE - **SYM-20W & SYM-22W**

SKY BUS EXPRESS - SKB
1994 - PRESENT
SOTHEAST US COMMUTER OPERATIONS

B. Shuey

SKB-10W
80MM BRITE GOLDTONE

B. Shuey

SKB-12W
80MM BRITE GOLDTONE

© PHILIP R. MARTIN 1995 ALL RIGHTS RESERVED. NO REPRODUCTION IN ANY FORM.

SKYWAYS - SYW
1953 - 1986
CENTRAL US COMMUTER OPERATIONS
- ORIGINALLY CALLED SCHEDULED SKYWAY SYSTEMS
- MERGED WITH AIR MIDWEST IN 1986,
  THEN CALLED AIR MIDWEST SKYWAYS,
  DROPPED SKYWAYS IN 1988

SYW-10W
68MM BRONZETONE WITH RED LOGO IN CENTER

SKYWEST - SKW
1972 - PRESENT
WESTERN US REGIONAL COMMUTER

SKW-10W
70MM SILVERTONE WITH BLACK CENTER

© PHILIP R. MARTIN 1995 ALL RIGHTS RESERVED. NO REPRODUCTION IN ANY FORM.

SLICK AIRWAYS - SLK
1946 - 1966
INTERNATIONAL AIR CARGO
• MERGED INTO AIRLIFT AIRLINES IN 1966

SLK-15B
STERLING or BRITE SILVERTONE WITH RED or DARK MAROON CENTER

Siracusa

SLK-12W
78MM STERLING or BRITE SILVERTONE WITH RED or DARK MAROON CENTER

Siracusa

SLK-15W
78MM STERLING or BRITE SILVERTONE WITH RED or DARK MAROON CENTER

© PHILIP R. MARTIN 1995 ALL RIGHTS RESERVED. NO REPRODUCTION IN ANY FORM.

SMB - SEE SEDALLIA-MARSHALL-BOONVILLE STAGE LINES LISTING

SOCONY OIL COMPANY - SOC
19XX - 19XX
INTERNATIONAL OIL COMPANY

SOC-10W
74MM SATIN GOLDTONE WITH LOGO

SOUTHERN AIR TRANSPORT - SAR
1928 - 1930
SOUTHERN US
• MERGED INTO AMERICAN AIRWAYS IN 1930

NATM/P

SOUTHERN AIR TRANSPORT - STA
1949 - PRESENT
MIAMI BASED CARRIBEAN AND LATIN AMERICA
• ORIGINALLY PRIVATELY OWNED • ACQUIRED BY THE CIA IN 1960
• CEASED WARTIME OPERATIONS AT THE END OF THE VIETNAM WAR

Koran

STA-10B
NATM • FLAT GOLDTONE

© PHILIP R. MARTIN 1995 ALL RIGHTS RESERVED. NO REPRODUCTION IN ANY FORM.

STA-20B
SILVERTONE WITH GREY
& BLACK LOGO CENTER

STA-20W
86MM SILVERTONE WITH GREY
& BLACK LOGO CENTER

STA-25W
86MM SILVERTONE WITH GREY & BLACK LOGO CENTER

SOUTHERN AIRWAYS - SAW
1949 - 1980
SOUTHERN US

- MERGED WITH NORTH CENTRAL AIRLINES
  TO FORM REPUBLIC AIRLINES IN 1980

SAW-10B
GOLDTONE "CAMP WOLTHERS, TEXAS"
<u>1949 - 1967</u>

SAW-1OW
49MM STERLING "BAINBRIDGE"
<u>1949 - 1967</u>

© PHILIP R. MARTIN 1995 ALL RIGHTS RESERVED. NO REPRODUCTION IN ANY FORM.

SAW-30B
GOLDTONE WITH BLUE CENTER
1949 - 1967

SAW-32W
64MM GOLDTONE WITH BLUE CENTER
1949 - 1967

SAW-40W
69MM STERLING, BLUE CENTER
1949 - 1967

SAW-52W
68MM STERLING
1949 - 1967

SAW-62W
68MM SILVERTONE, BLUE CENTER
1949 - 1967

SAW-72W
68MM GOLDTONE, BLUE CENTER
1949 - 1967

© PHILIP R. MARTIN 1995 ALL RIGHTS RESERVED. NO REPRODUCTION IN ANY FORM.

SAW-70B
FLAT SILVERTONE
<u>1967 - 1972</u>

SAW-72W
69MM FLAT SILVERTONE
<u>1967 - 1972</u>

SAW-75W
69MM FLAT SILVERTONE
<u>1967 - 1972</u>

SAW-80B
BRITE/FLAT GOLDTONE,
LOGO IN BLUE CENTER
<u>1967 - 1972</u>

SAW-82W
68MM BRITE/FLAT GOLDTONE,
LOGO IN BLUE CENTER
<u>1972 - 1980</u>

SAW- 85W
68MM BRITE/FLAT GOLDTONE,
LOGO IN BLUE CENTER
<u>1972 - 1980</u>

© PHILIP R. MARTIN 1995 ALL RIGHTS RESERVED. NO REPRODUCTION IN ANY FORM.

SOUTH PACIFIC ISLANDS AIRWAYS - SPI
1973 - PRESENT
AMERICAN SAMOA - SOUTH PACIFIC

SPI-10W
79MM BRITE SILVERTONE WITH WHITE BIRD ON
GREEN & DARK BLUE CIRCLE, PATTERN & LETTERS

SOUTHWEST AIR FAST EXPRESS - SWX
1929 - 1930
MID-SOUTH US
• CEASED OPERATIONS IN 1930

NATM/P

SOUTHWEST AIRLINES - SWA
1946 - 1968
PACIFIC COAST- US
• CHANGED NAME TO PACIFIC AIR LINES IN 1958
• MERGED WITH BONANZA AIRLINES AND WEST COAST AIRLINES
TO FORM AIR WEST IN 1968
• MERGER SUBSEQUENTLY BECAME HUGHES AIR WEST IN 1970

NATM/P

© PHILIP R. MARTIN 1995 ALL RIGHTS RESERVED. NO REPRODUCTION IN ANY FORM.

SOUTHWEST AIRLINES - SWS
1971 - PRESENT
REGIONAL CARRIER - WESTERN US

SWS-10B
BRITE SILVERTONE

SWS-10W
68MM BRITE SILVERTONE

SWS-12W
68MM BRITE SILVERTONE
CAPTAIN

SWS-15W
68MM BRITE SILVERTONE
CHECK AIRMAN

SOUTHWEST AIRWAYS - SWW
1946 - 1958
CALIFORNIA - OREGON
REGIONAL
• CHANGED NAME TO PACIFIC AIRLINES IN 1958

SWW-10W Koran
NATM • GOLDTONE, BLACK CENTER, LOGO

© PHILIP R. MARTIN 1995 ALL RIGHTS RESERVED. NO REPRODUCTION IN ANY FORM.

STANDARD AIR LINES - STD
1927 - 1930
L.A.-TUSCON-EL PASO
• MERGED INTO WESTERN AIR EXPRESS IN 1930 • LATER MERGED INTO AMERICAN AIRWAYS

STD-10W
91MM BLACK CLOTH WITH GOLD BULLION,
LIGHT GREEN CENTER WITH GOLD LETTERS

STAR AIR LINES - STR
1938 - 1943
ALASKA
• MERGED INTO ALASKA AIRLINES IN 1943

NATM/P

STAR AIR SERVICE - STS
1932 - 1938
ALASKA
• MERGED INTO STAR AIR LINES IN 1938

NATM/P

STATEWIDE AIRLINES - STW
1964 - 1967
NEW YORK REGIONAL
• MERGED INTO TRANS-EAST AIRLINES IN 1967

NATM/P

© PHILIP R. MARTIN 1995 ALL RIGHTS RESERVED. NO REPRODUCTION IN ANY FORM.

STOUT AIR SERVICES - STO
1926 -1928
GREAT LAKES REGIONAL
- MERGED INTO UNITED AIR LINES WITH FORD MOTOR CO. IN 1929

NATM/P

SUBURBAN AIRLINES - SBN
1968 - PRESENT
EAST AND NORTHEAST US COMMUTER

- BEGAN IN 1957 AS READING AIRLINES
- CHANGED NAME TO SUBURBAN AIRLINES IN 1968
- OPERATED AS ALLEGHENY COMMUTER, LATER AS US AIR EXPRESS

NATM/P

SUMMIT AIRWAYS - SUM
1945 - 1949
MID WEST US
- MERGED INTO FRONTIER AIRLINES IN 1950

NATM/P

SUN AIRE LINES - SUN
1967 - 1987
SOUTHWEST US COMMUTER
- ABSORBED INTO PARENT COMPANY, SKYWEST IN 1987

NATM/P

SUN COUNTRY AIRLINES - SCX
1982 - PRESENT
MIDWEST US CHARTER CARRIER

NATM/P

© PHILIP R. MARTIN 1995 ALL RIGHTS RESERVED. NO REPRODUCTION IN ANY FORM.

SUN JET AIRLINES - SNJ
1994 - PRESENT
FLORIDA BASED US CHARTER AND REGIONAL

SNJ-10B
BRITE GOLDTONE, BLUE CENTER, YELLOW & ORANGE LOGO

SNJ-12W
84 MM BRITE GOLDTONE, BLUE
CENTER, YELLOW & ORANGE

SNJ-15W
84 MM BRITE GOLDTONE, BLUE
CENTER, YELLOW & ORANGE

SUN WEST AIRLINES - SNW
1979 - PRESENT
SOUTHWEST US COMMUTER

NATM/P

© PHILIP R. MARTIN 1995 ALL RIGHTS RESERVED. NO REPRODUCTION IN ANY FORM.

SUNBIRD AIRLINES - SBD
1979 - 1987

US EAST COAST AND SOUTH COMMUTER
• MERGED WITH ATLANTA EXPRESS AIRLINE IN 1983 • RE-EMERGED AS SUNBIRD AFTER
ATLANTA EXPRESS FAILED IN 1983 • CHANGED NAME TO CC AIR IN 1987

NATM/P

SUNWORLD INTERNATIONAL AIRWAYS - SWO
1981 - PRESENT

SOUTHWEST US REGIONAL CARRIER
• ORIGINALLY ESTABLISHED AS
JETWEST INTERNATIONAL AIRWAYS

NATM/P

SUSQUEHANNA AIRLINES - SQH
1971 - 1987

NORTHEAST US COMMUTER
• OUT OF BUSINESS IN 1987

NATM/P

SUPERIOR AIRLINES - SUP
1960 - 1962

SOUTHERN - US
• ALPA OWNED AIRLINE IN COMPETITION WITH SOUTHERN AIRWAYS
• CEASED OPERATIONS IN 1962

NATM/P

SWIFT AIRE LINES - SWF
1969 - 1981

CENTRAL & SOUTHERN CALIFORNIA COMMUTER
• CEASED OPERATIONS IN 1981

NATM/P

© PHILIP R. MARTIN 1995 ALL RIGHTS RESERVED. NO REPRODUCTION IN ANY FORM.

SWIFT AIR SERVICE - SAS
1985
CENTRAL & SOUTHERN CALIFORNIA COMMUTER
• STARTED & CEASED OPERATIONS IN 1985

SAS-12B
SATIN GOLDTONE WITH WHITE CONTINENT IN BLACK CIRCLE

SAS-12W
70MM SATIN GOLDTONE WITH WHITE CONTINENT IN BLACK CIRCLE

© PHILIP R. MARTIN 1995 ALL RIGHTS RESERVED. NO REPRODUCTION IN ANY FORM.

T

TAG AIRLINES (TAXI AIR GROUP) - TAG
1958 - 1965
MICHIGAN - OHIO
• OUT OF BUSINESS IN 1965

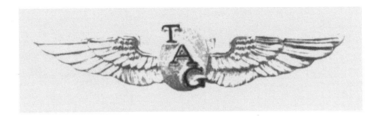

TAG-10W
69MM BRITE GOLDTONE
Made from a 1950's US Navy Flight Surgeon Wing

TEXAS AIR TRANSPORT - TXT
1927 - 1928
SOUTHERN US
• MERGED INTO SOUTHERN AIRLINES IN 1928

NATM/P

TEXAS INTERNATIONAL AIRLINES - TXI
1969 - 1982
SOUTHERN US REGIONAL CARRIER
• EVOLVED FROM TRANS TEXAS AIRLINES IN 1970
• MERGED WITH CONTINENTAL AIRLINES IN 1982

TXI-10B
STERLING
1968 - 1972

TXI-10W
84MM STERLING
1968 - 1972

© PHILIP R. MARTIN 1995 ALL RIGHTS RESERVED. NO REPRODUCTION IN ANY FORM.

TXI-12W
84MM STERLING
1968 - 1972

TXI-15W
84MM STERLING
1968 - 1972

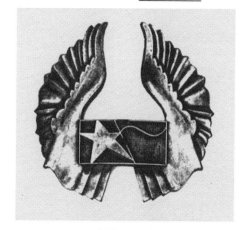

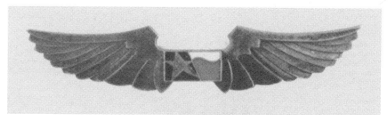

TXI-20B
STERLING & TEXAS FLAG (NO COLOR)
1972 - 1982

TXI-20W
84MM STERLING & 3 COLOR TEXAS FLAG
1972 - 1982

TXI-25W
84MM STERLING & 3 COLOR TEXAS FLAG
1972 - 1982

© PHILIP R. MARTIN 1995 ALL RIGHTS RESERVED. NO REPRODUCTION IN ANY FORM.

TOWER AIR - TOW
1982 - PRESENT
INTERNATIONAL CHARTER CARRIER

NATM / P

TRANSAMERICA AIRLINES - TIA
1979 - 1986
NATIONAL CARRIER

- EVOLVED FROM TRANS INTERNATIONAL AIRLINES IN 1968
- CHANGED NAME TO TRANSAMERICA IN 1979
- AFFILIATED WITH INSURANCE COMPANY
- CEASED OPERATIONS IN 1986

TIA-10B
84 MM GREYTONE,
GREEN LOGO CENTER

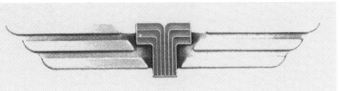

TIA-10W
84 MM GREYTONE,
GREEN LOGO CENTER

TIA-15W
84 MM GREYTONE, GREEN LOGO CENTER

© PHILIP R. MARTIN 1995 ALL RIGHTS RESERVED. NO REPRODUCTION IN ANY FORM.

TIA-20W
80MM BRITE GOLDTONE
WITH LOGO IN RED CENTER

TIA-22W
80MM BRITE GOLDTONE
WITH LOGO IN RED CENTER

TIA-25W
80MM BRITE GOLDTONE WITH LOGO IN RED CENTER

TRANSAMERICAN AIRLINES CORP. - TAC
1928 - 1932

NORTH CENTRAL US - GREAT LAKES AREA
• MERGED INTO AMERICAN AIRWAYS IN 1932

Joiner

TRA-10W
NATM • FLAT GOLDTONE

© PHILIP R. MARTIN 1995 ALL RIGHTS RESERVED. NO REPRODUCTION IN ANY FORM.

TRANS AMERICAN AIRLINES - TAA
1979 - 1986
INTERNATIONAL

TAA-10W
72MM BRITE GOLD FILLED

TRANSCONTINENTAL AIR TRANSPORT - TAT
1928 - 1930
US
• MERGED WITH WESTERN AIR EXPRESS IN 1930

C. Weeks

TAT-10W
NATM • GOLDTONE

© PHILIP R. MARTIN 1995 ALL RIGHTS RESERVED. NO REPRODUCTION IN ANY FORM.

TRANSCONTINENTAL & WESTERN AIR - TCW
1930 - 1950
WORLDWIDE
- FORMED OUT OF A MERGER OF TRANSCONTINENTAL AIR TRANSPORT AND A PART OF WESTERN AIR EXPRESS IN 1930
- CHANGED ITS NAME TO TRANS WORLD AIRLINES IN 1950

TCW-10B
BRONZETONE

TCW-10W
85MM BRONZETONE

C. Weeks

TCW-20B
SATIN GOLDTONE

TCW-20W
82MM SATIN GOLDTONE

© PHILIP R. MARTIN 1995 ALL RIGHTS RESERVED. NO REPRODUCTION IN ANY FORM.

TRANSOCEAN AIR LINES - TRO
1948 - 1960
GUAM-MICRONESIA & WORLDWIDE CHARTER CARRIER
- CEASED OPERATIONS IN 1960

TR0-10B
STERLING WITH GOLD CENTER

TR0-10W
93MM STERLING WITH 2 GOLD STARS
NAVIGATOR, FLIGHT ENGINEER or RADIO OFFICER

TR0-12W
93MM STERLING, 3 GOLD STARS
FIRST OFFICER

TR0-15W
93MM STERLING, 4 GOLD STARS
CAPTAIN

TR0-20B
STERLING, GF CENTER

TR0-20W
93MM STERLING

© PHILIP R. MARTIN 1995 ALL RIGHTS RESERVED. NO REPRODUCTION IN ANY FORM.

TRANSTAR - TRS
1985 - 1987
SOUTHWEST US
- ACQUIRED BY SOUTHWEST AIRLINES IN 1985
- CHANGED NAME FROM MUSE AIR
- OPERATED AS AN INDEPENDENT SUBSIDIARY

TRS-10B
SATIN BRONZETONE
WITH BLACK/GREEN BAR

TRS-10W
82MM SATIN BRONZETONE
WITH BLACK/GREEN BAR

TRS-12W
82MM SATIN BRONZETONE WITH BLACK/GREEN BAR

L. Ginsburg

TRS-15W
82MM SATIN BRONZETONE WITH BLACK/GREEN BAR

© PHILIP R. MARTIN 1995 ALL RIGHTS RESERVED. NO REPRODUCTION IN ANY FORM.

TRANS CARIBBEAN AIRWAYS - TRC
1945 - 1971
SOUTHERN US & CARIBBEAN
• MERGED INTO AMERICAN AIRLINES IN 1971

NATM/P

TRANS CONTINENTAL AIRLINES - TCN
1972 - 1986
MICHIGAN

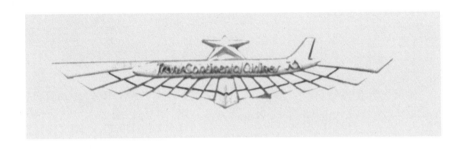

TCN-12W
74MM SATIN SILVERTONE

TRANS FLORIDA AIRLINES - TFA
1966 - PRESENT
SOUTHEAST US

TFA-30W
78MM SATIN GOLDTONE WITH BLUE LETTERS ON WHITE DISC

© PHILIP R. MARTIN 1995 ALL RIGHTS RESERVED. NO REPRODUCTION IN ANY FORM.

TRANS GLOBAL AIRLINES - TGA
1982 - 19XX
UNKNOWN
UNKNOWN

TGA-12W
78MM SATIN/BRITE GOLDTONE,
LETTERS ON BLUE CENTER

TGA-15W
78MM SATIN/BRITE GOLDTONE,
LETTERS ON BLUE CENTER

TRANS INTERNATIONAL AIRLINES - TRI
1960 - 1979
US & TRANSATLANTIC
• ORIGINALLY FORMED AS LOS ANGELES AIR SERVICE IN 1948
• CHANGED NAME TO TRANS INTERNATIONAL AIRLINES IN 1960
• ABSORBED SATURN AIRWAYS IN 1976
• CHANGED INTO TRANSAMERICA AIRLINES 1979

TRI-10B
FLAT SILVERTONE,
LIGHT BLUE CENTER

TRI-10W
72MM FLAT SILVERTONE,
LIGHT BLUE CENTER

© PHILIP R. MARTIN 1995 ALL RIGHTS RESERVED. NO REPRODUCTION IN ANY FORM.

TRI-15W
72MM FLAT SILVERTONE WITH
LIGHT BLUE CENTER

TRI-20B
FLAT GREYTONE,
LIGHT GREEN CENTER

TRI-20W
75MM FLAT GREYTONE WITH
LIGHT GREEN CENTER

TRI-25W
75MM FLAT GREYTONE WITH
LIGHT GREEN CENTER

TRANS PACIFIC AIRLINES - TPA
1946 - 1959
HAWAII - PACIFIC REGION
• CHANGED NAME TO ALOHA AIRLINES IN 1959

TPA-10B
SATIN GOLDTONE "KING KAMEHAMEHA"

TPA-10W
71MM SATIN GOLDTONE "KING KAMEHAMEHA"

© PHILIP R. MARTIN 1995 ALL RIGHTS RESERVED. NO REPRODUCTION IN ANY FORM.

TRANS STATES AIRLINES - LOF
19 XX - PRESENT
- UNKNOWN

NATM/P

TRANS TEXAS AIRWAYS - TTA
1947 - 1969
SOUTHWEST US
- FOUNDED AS AVIATION ENTERPRISES IN 1944
- CHANGED NAME TO TEXAS INTERNATIONAL IN 1969

TTA-10B
STERLING WITH TEXAS STATE
OUTLINE AND BIRD

TTA-20B
GOLDTONE OVER STERLING WITH
TEXAS STATE OUTLINE AND BIRD

TTA-10W
83MM STERLING WITH TEXAS STATE OUTLINE AND BIRD

TTA-12W
83MM STERLING WITH TEXAS STATE OUTLINE AND BIRD

© PHILIP R. MARTIN 1995 ALL RIGHTS RESERVED. NO REPRODUCTION IN ANY FORM.

TRANS WORLD AIRLINES (TWA) - TWA
1950 - PRESENT
WORLDWIDE

- EVOLVED FROM TRANSCONTENTAL & WESTERN AIR-
  (A MERGER OF WESTERN AIR EXPRESS, TRANSCONTINENTAL
  AIR TRANSPORT & PITTSBURG AVIATION INDUSTRIES)
- WESTERN AIR EXPRESS WITHDRAWS IN 1941
- CHANGED NAME TO TRANS WORLD AIRLINES IN 1950

C.Weeks

TWA-15W
80MM SATIN BRONZETONE

TWA-11B
STERLING FA PIN, RED INLAY

TWA-20W
84MM SATIN GOLDTONE

TWA-25W
84MM SATIN GOLDTONE

TWA-30B
84MM SATIN 1/20 GOLD FILLED

TWA-30W
84MM SATIN 1/20 GOLD FILLED
"CAREER FLIGHT ENGINEER"

© PHILIP R. MARTIN 1995 ALL RIGHTS RESERVED. NO REPRODUCTION IN ANY FORM.

TWA-31W
84MM SATIN 1/20 GOLD FILLED
FLIGHT ENGINEER ON TRACK FOR CAPTAIN

TWA-35W
84MM SATIN 1/20 GOLD FILLED
CAPTAIN

TRANS WORLD EXPRESS - MNE
1985 - PRESENT
TWA COMMUTER
- ALSO KNOWN AS METRO NORTHEAST
- AIR MIDWEST, KANSAS FROM 1986 - PRESENT
- RESORT AIR, MISSOURI FROM 1985 -
- RESORT COMMUTER AIRLINE, CALIFORNIA FROM 1986 - 19XX
- RANSOME AIRLINES (PAN AM EXPRESS),
  THEN TWA OWNED COMMUTER IN 1991

B. Shuey

MNE-10W
77MM SATIN GOLDTONE, BLACK/RED
CENTER AND GOLD LETTERS

MNE-25W
NATM • GOLDTONE, RED LETTERS

© PHILIP R. MARTIN 1995 ALL RIGHTS RESERVED. NO REPRODUCTION IN ANY FORM.

TRUMP EXPRESS - TPS
1990 - 1993
EAST COAST US COMMUTER (SHUTTLE)
• PURCHASED EASTERN AIRLINES NORTHEAST CORRIDOR ROUTES
• ASSETS SOLD TO US AIR

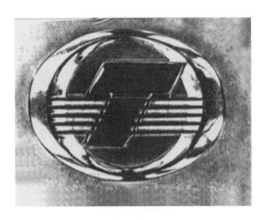

TPS-10B
NATM • GOLDTONE, RED "T"

D. Kerr

TPS-12W
NATM • BRITE GOLDTONE WITH RED "T"

TPS-15W
NATM • BRITE GOLDTONE WITH RED "T"

© PHILIP R. MARTIN 1995 ALL RIGHTS RESERVED. NO REPRODUCTION IN ANY FORM.

TURNER AIRLINES (ROSCOE TURNER AIRLINES) - TUR
1946 - 1949
INDIANA
• MERGED INTO LAKE CENTRAL AIRLINES IN 1950

K. Boyer

TUR-10W
116MM STERLING WITH BLACK LETTERS

NOTE THE LARGE SIZE OF THE TURNER WING.
MOST OF THEIR PILOTS REFUSED TO WEAR THE LARGE, FLASHY WING BECAUSE IT JABBED THEM IN THE ARM WHILE MOVING AROUND THE COCKPIT.

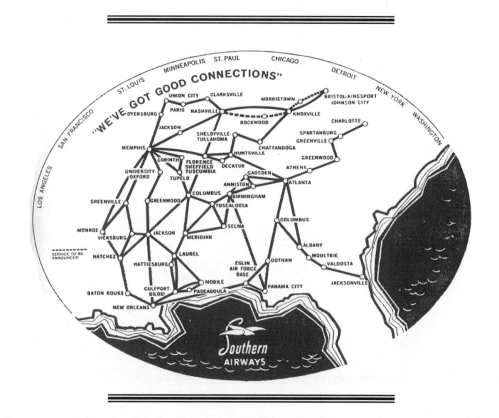

© PHILIP R. MARTIN 1995 ALL RIGHTS RESERVED. NO REPRODUCTION IN ANY FORM.

U

ULTRAIR - UAT
1992 - PRESENT
US CARGO AND CHARTER CARRIER

UAT-10B
BRITE COPPERTONE

UAT-10W
72MM BRITE COPPERTONE

UNITED AIRCRAFT & TRANSPORT - UAT
1928 - 1931
US
- MERGED INTO UNITED AIRLINES IN 1931

NATM/P

UNITED AIRLINES (UAL) - UAL
1931 - PRESENT
WORLDWIDE
- EVOLVED FROM A MERGER OF NATIONAL AIR TRANSPORT, BOEING AIR TRANSPORT AND UNITED AIRCRAFT & TRANSPORT IN 1931

UAL-10W (SEE USM-10W)
86MM GOLD OR ROLLED GOLD
BULLION "US AIR MAIL"

UAL-20B
BLACK CLOTH WITH SILVER
"UNITED" ON A RED, WHITE & BLUE SHEILD

© PHILIP R. MARTIN 1995 ALL RIGHTS RESERVED. NO REPRODUCTION IN ANY FORM.

Note the position of the words & symbols, and the "wavy" bands above and the straight lines in the wing on the right.

UAL-20W
NATM/ BLACK CLOTH WITH SILVER BULLION SILVER "UNITED" ON A RED, ON A RED, WHITE & BLUE SHIELD

UAL-30W
88MM BLACK CLOTH WITH SILVER BULLION "UNITED" WHITE & BLUE SHEILD

UAL-40W
86MM STERLING RED, WHITE & BLUE SHEILD
<u>1956 - 1979</u>

UAL-50W
86MM STERLING
<u>1956 - 1979</u>

© PHILIP R. MARTIN 1995 ALL RIGHTS RESERVED. NO REPRODUCTION IN ANY FORM.

UAL-60B
STERLING OR GOLDTONE
1979 - PRESENT
USED EARLY IN SILVERTONE WITH A BLACK LEATHER BACKING, LATER DURING A UNIFORM CHANGE IT CHANGED TO GOLDTONE WITH A BROWN LEATHER BACKING. A WREATH APPEARS AT THE BOTTOM FOR SENIOR AIRMEN.

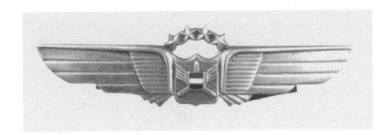

UAL-62W
64MM STERLING GOLDTONE
1956 - PRESENT

UAL-65W
86MM BRITE GOLDTONE
1979 - PRESENT

EACH DIAMOND CHIP IS ADDED TO STARS ON WREATH <u>ABOVE</u> AT 5 YEARS OF SERVICE.
CHECK AIRMAN HAS WREATH <u>BELOW</u> CENTER.
DIAMOND IS ADDED TO WREATH <u>BELOW</u> FOR CHECK AIRMAN WITH 25 YEARS OF SERVICE.

© PHILIP R. MARTIN 1995 ALL RIGHTS RESERVED. NO REPRODUCTION IN ANY FORM.

UNITED EXPRESS - NPE
1986 - PRESENT
UNITED AIRLINES REGIONAL COMMUTERS
CONSISTING OF :
- AIR WISCONSIN, FROM 1986 - PRESENT
- ASPEN AIRWAYS, COLORADO FROM 1986 - 1991
- NPA, WASHINGTON FROM 1987 - 1990
- PRESIDENTIAL AIRLINES, D.C. FROM 1988 - 1989
- PRESIDENTIAL EXPRESS, VIRGINIA FROM 1988 - 19XX
- WESTAIR, CALIFORNIA FROM 1986 - PRESENT

CHECK EACH AIRLINE LISTING

UNITED PARCEL SERVICE - UPS
1988 - PRESENT
INTERNATIONAL AIR CARGO CARRIER
- BEGAN AIR OPERATIONS BY CONTRACTING WITH OTHER AIR CARGO COMPANIES
- STARTED THEIR OWN AIR CARGO OPERATION IN 1988

UPS-10B
BRITE GOLDTONE WITH
UPS LOGO IN BROWN CENTER

UPS-10W
71MM BRITE GOLDTONE WITH
UPS LOGO IN BROWN CENTER

UPS-12B
BRITE GOLDTONE WITH
UPS LOGO IN BROWN CENTER

UPS-12W
71MM BRITE GOLDTONE WITH
UPS LOGO IN BROWN CENTER

© PHILIP R. MARTIN 1995 ALL RIGHTS RESERVED. NO REPRODUCTION IN ANY FORM.

UNITED STATES AIRWAYS - USA
1929 - 1934
MID US
• CEASED OPERATIONS IN 1934

NATM/P

UNITED STATES GOVERNMENT - SAM
1930 - PRESENT
GOVERNMENTAL AGENCIES

SAM-10W
72MM SATIN GOLDTONE
FOREST SERVICE PILOT

SAM-20W
52MM FLAT GOLDTONE
FAA ATC CONTROLLER

THESE ARE ONLY TWO EXAMPLES OF U.S. GOVT. ISSUE WINGS
IT IS NOT CLEAR HOW MANY AGENCIES HAVE THEIR OWN WINGS.
ALSO PLEASE CHECK THE CAA LISTING.

UNITED STATES OVERSEAS AIRLINES (USOA) - USO
1946 - 1964
US
• CEASED OPERATIONS IN 1964

USO-10W
87MM STERLING

© PHILIP R. MARTIN 1995 ALL RIGHTS RESERVED. NO REPRODUCTION IN ANY FORM.

UNIVERSAL AIRLINES - UNI
1966 - 1972
US-AIR CARGO
- FOUNDED AS ZANTOP AIR TRANSPORT IN 1956
- CHANGED NAME TO UNIVERSAL AIRLINES IN 1966
- PURCHASED AMERICAN FLYERS AIRLINE IN 1971
- CEASED OPERATIONS IN 1972

UNI-12W
75MM FLAT SILVERTONE WITH BLUE GLOBE IN CENTER

UNIVERSAL AVIATION CORP. - UNA
1928 - 1930
- MERGED INTO AMERICAN AIRWAYS IN 1930

NATM/P

US AIR - USA
1979 - PRESENT
US
- EVOLVED FROM ALLEGHENY AIRLINES IN 1979
- MERGED WITH PACIFIC SOUTHWEST AIRLINES IN 1988
- MERGED WITH PIEDMONT AIRLINES IN 1989

USA-10W
80MM STERLING MAROON LETTERS

USA-12W
80MM STERLING MAROON LETTERS

© PHILIP R. MARTIN 1995 ALL RIGHTS RESERVED. NO REPRODUCTION IN ANY FORM.

USA-15W
80MM STERLING MAROON LETTERS

USA-20B
SATIN/BRITE SILVERTONE WITH
RED "US" & LT.BLUE "AIR"

USA-20W
80MM SATIN/BRITE SILVERTONE
WITH RED "US" & LT.BLUE "AIR"

USA-25W
80MM SATIN/BRITE SILVERTONE
WITH RED "US" & LT.BLUE "AIR"

US AIR EXPRESS - USX
SEE ALLEGHENY COMMUTER FOR PRIOR AND CURRENT LISTINGS
REGIONAL COMMUTER SYSTEM

USX-10W
80MM FLAT SILVERTONE,
RED & BLUE LETTERS

USX-15W
80MM FLAT SILVERTONE
RED & BLUE LETTERS

© PHILIP R. MARTIN 1995 ALL RIGHTS RESERVED. NO REPRODUCTION IN ANY FORM.

US AIR SHUTTLE - USS
1994 - PRESENT
EASTERN US REGIONAL COMMUTER SYSTEM

NATM/P

US AIR MAIL - USA
1928 - 1939
EARLY AIR MAIL CARRIERS
• GRADUALLY MAIL CONTRACTS WERE GIVEN TO SPECIFIC AIR CARRIERS

USM-10W
86MM GOLD

USM-20W
82MM STERLING GOLD FILLED

SEE NORTHWEST AIRLINES LISTING FOR PRESENT USE
SEE DELTA AIRLINES AND UNITED AIR LINES LISTING FOR PAST USE
SEE COLOR PLATES

US AIRLINES - USL
1949 - 1955
REGIONAL AIR CARGO CARRIER
• MERGED INTO EASTERN AIRLINES IN 1955

NATM/P

© PHILIP R. MARTIN 1995 ALL RIGHTS RESERVED. NO REPRODUCTION IN ANY FORM.

V

VAIL AIRWAYS - VAI
1964 - 1968
ROCKY MOUNTAIN AREA COMMUTER
• CHANGED NAME TO ROCKY MTS, AIRWAYS IN 1968

NATM/P

VALUJET AIRLINES - VAL
1994 - PRESENT
SOUTHERN US
ATLANTA BASED COMMUTER

VAL-10W
79MM BRITE GOLDTONE, BLUE, WHITE & YELLOW CENTER

VARNEY AIR LINES - VAR
1926 - 1933
WESTERN US
• MERGED INTO BOEING AIR TRANSPORT, THEN A DIVISION OF UNITED AIRLINES

NATM/P

VARNEY AIR TRANSPORT - VAT
1934 - 1937
SOUTHWEST US
• PURCHASED ROUTES FROM WYOMING AIR SERVICE IN 1937
• RENAMED CONTINENTAL AIR LINES IN 1937

NATM/P

© PHILIP R. MARTIN 1995 ALL RIGHTS RESERVED. NO REPRODUCTION IN ANY FORM.

VARNEY SPEED LINES - VSL
1933 - 1937
CALIFORNIA-WESTERN US
• REORGANIZED INTO CONTINENTAL AIR LINES IN 1937

NATM/P

VIKING AIR LINES - VIK
1945 - 1947
CALIFORNIA AIR CARGO CARRIER
• MERGED INTO OXNARD AIR CARGO

VIK-10W
80 MM BRITE SILVERTONE

VIKING INTERNATIONAL AIRLINES - VIA
1969 - 19XX
CORPORATE CHARTER

NATM/P

© PHILIP R. MARTIN 1995 ALL RIGHTS RESERVED. NO REPRODUCTION IN ANY FORM.

W

WEST AIR - WES
1972 - PRESENT
REGIONAL COMMUTER
- STARTED AS STOL AIR IN 1972 • SEPERATED FROM PACIFIC EXPRESS IN 1983
- OPERATES NOW AS A UNITED EXPRESS COMMUTER

WES-10W
77MM BRITE/SATIN SILVERTONE

WEST COAST AIRLINES - WCA
1946 - 1967
WESTERN US
- JOINED WITH BONANZA AIRLINES AND PACIFIC COAST AIRLINE TO FORM AIR WEST IN 1967

WCA-10B
STERLING, GREEN LETTERS

WCA-10W
88MM STERLING, GREEN LETTERS

© PHILIP R. MARTIN 1995 ALL RIGHTS RESERVED. NO REPRODUCTION IN ANY FORM.

WEST COAST AIR TRANSPORT - WCT
1927-1930
WESTERN US
• BOUGHT BY WESTERN AIR EXPRESS IN 1930

NATM/P

WESTERN AIR EXPRESS (WAE) - WAE
1925 - 1941
WESTERN US
• ONE PORTION OF WAE MERGED WITH TAT TO FORM TRANSCONTINENTAL & WORLD AIRLINES IN 1930
• ANOTHER PORTION, ORIGINALLY NATIONAL PARKS AIRWAYS, CONTINUED ON AS WAE
• CHANGED NAME TO WESTERN AIRLINES IN 1941

S.D.A.M.

WAE-10W
87MM BLACK CLOTH, SILVER BULLION, LIGHT BLUE HEAD ON WHITE DISC
"WAE" ON HEADBAND

J. Joiner

WAE-20B
GOLDTONE, RED LETTERS

S..D..A..M.

WAE-20W
86 MM GOLDTONE - NUMBERED

© PHILIP R. MARTIN 1995 ALL RIGHTS RESERVED. NO REPRODUCTION IN ANY FORM.

WESTERN AIRLINES - WAL
1941 - 1986
US

- GENERAL MOTORS BUYS STOCK IN 1940'S
- MERGED WITH DELTA AIRLINES IN 1986

WAL-10B
GOLDTONE - SMALL
INDIAN HEAD FACING LEFT

WAL-10W
65MM BRITE GOLDTONE - LARGE
INDIAN HEAD FACING RIGHT

J. Joiner

WAL-20B
GOLDTONE - SMALL
INDIAN HEAD FACING LEFT

WAL-20W
71MM GOLDTONE - SMALL
INDIAN HEAD FACING LEFT

© PHILIP R. MARTIN 1995 ALL RIGHTS RESERVED. NO REPRODUCTION IN ANY FORM.

WAL-22B
SILVERTONE - SMALL INDIAN
HEAD FACING LEFT - NAME ABOVE

WAL-30B
STERLING - SMALL INDIAN
HEAD FACING RIGHT IN OVAL

WAL-30W
73MM STERLING - SMALL INDIAN
HEAD FACING RIGHT IN OVAL

WAL-40B
STERLING "W" IN SQUARE CENTER

WAL-40W
72MM STERLING "W" IN SQUARE

WAL-45W
72MM STERLING "W" IN SQUARE

© PHILIP R. MARTIN 1995 ALL RIGHTS RESERVED. NO REPRODUCTION IN ANY FORM.

WIEN AIR ALASKA - WAA
1973 - 1984
ALASKA & CONTINENTAL US
- FORMED FROM WIEN CONSOLIDATED IN 1973
- OUT OF BUSINESS IN 1984

WAA-10B
STERLING WITH BLUE CENTER

WAA-10W
76MM STERLING WITH BLUE CENTER

WAA-15W
76MM STERLING WITH BLUE CENTER

© PHILIP R. MARTIN 1995 ALL RIGHTS RESERVED. NO REPRODUCTION IN ANY FORM.

WIEN CONSOLIDATED AIRLINES - WIC
1932 - 1973
ALASKA- WEST COAST US
• BEGAN AS WIEN AIRWAYS OF ALASKA IN 1932 • MERGED WITH NORTHERN CONSOLIDATED AIRLINES IN 1968
• CHANGED NAME TO WIEN AIR ALASKA IN 1973

NATM/P

WILMINGTON-CATALINA AIRLINE - WIL
1931 - 1942
CATALINA
• MERGED INTO CATALINA AIR TRANSPORT IN 1942

NATM/P

WINGS AIRWAYS - WAW

1976 - 1988
EASTERN US COMMUTER OPERATIONS
• OUT OF BUSINESS IN 1988

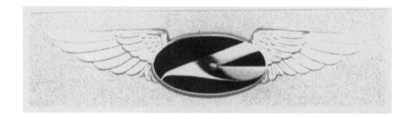

WAW-10W
71MM SATIN/BRITE SILVERTONE WITH BLUE CENTER

WINGS OF ALASKA - WIA
1983 - 19XX
ALASKA REGIONAL COMMUTER & SIGHTSEEING
• BEGAN AS SOUTHEAST SKYWAYS IN 1968
• CHANGED ITS NAME TO AIR AMERICA IN 1982
• CHANGED ITS NAME TO WINGS OF ALASKA IN 1983

NATM/P

WINGS WEST AIRLINES - WWA
1979 - PRESENT
CALIFORNIA COMMUTER
• BECAME AMERICAN EAGLE COMMUTER IN 1986

WWA-10W
70MM SATIN/BRITE SILVERTONE

WWA-20W
70MM SATIN/BRITE SILVERTONE,
GREEN LOGO IN CENTER

WISCONSIN CENTRAL AIRLINES - WIS
1948 - 1952
MID-WEST, GREAT LAKES US
• RENAMED NORTH CENTRAL AIRLINES IN 1952

WIS-10B
75MM STERLING WITH BLUE
RING AND RED CENTER, 4 STARS

WIS-10W
75MM STERLING WITH BLUE
RING AND RED CENTER

© PHILIP R. MARTIN 1995 ALL RIGHTS RESERVED. NO REPRODUCTION IN ANY FORM.

WORLD AIRWAYS - WOA
1948 - PRESENT
INTERNATIONAL AIR CARGO & CHARTER

WOA-10W
98MM BLACK CLOTH WITH RED
& SILVER CENTER LOGO

WOA-12W
98MM BLACK CLOTH WITH RED
& SILVER CENTER LOGO

WOA-20W
78MM BRITE GOLDTONE, RED LOGO

WOA-22W
78MM BRITE GOLDTONE, RED LOGO

WOA-25W
78MM BRITE GOLDTONE, RED LOGO

WOA-30W
84MM BRITE GOLDTONE & LOGO

© PHILIP R. MARTIN 1995 ALL RIGHTS RESERVED. NO REPRODUCTION IN ANY FORM.

WOA-32W	WOA-35W
84MM BRITE GOLDTONE & LOGO	84MM BRITE GOLDTONE & LOGO

WRIGHT AIR LINES - WRT
1966 - 1985
MID-WEST REGIONAL CARRIER-US
• OUT OF BUSINESS IN 1985

NATM/P

WYOMING AIR SERVICE - WYM
1931 - 1943
CENTRAL US
• MERGED INTO WESTERN AIRLINES IN 1943

NATM/P

© PHILIP R. MARTIN 1995 ALL RIGHTS RESERVED. NO REPRODUCTION IN ANY FORM.

X

XEROX CORPORATION - XER
19 XX - PRESENT
INTERNATIONAL CORPORATION

XER-10B
SATIN GOLDTONE

XER-10W
84MM SATIN GOLDTONE

Y

YOUNGSTOWN AIRLINES- YOU
19 XX -19 XX
•"WORLD'S LARGEST EXECUTIVE FLEET"

YOU-10W
80MM BRITE / SATIN GOLDTONE

© PHILIP R. MARTIN 1995 ALL RIGHTS RESERVED. NO REPRODUCTION IN ANY FORM.

YUTE AIR ALASKA - YAA
1963 - PRESENT
ALASKAN REGIONAL COMMUTER

NATM/P

Z

ZANTOP AIRLINES - ZNA
1956 - 1966
AIR CARGO
• SOLD TO UNIVERSAL AIRLINES IN 1966

NATM/P

ZANTOP AIR TRANSPORT - ZNT
1981 - 19XX
AIR CARGO CARRIER
• CHANGED NAME TO "INTERNATIONAL"

ZNT-15W
98MM BLACK CLOTH, SILVER BULLION, RED & WHITE THREAD

© PHILIP R. MARTIN 1995 ALL RIGHTS RESERVED. NO REPRODUCTION IN ANY FORM.

ZNT-20W
86MM STERLING WITH RED
LETTERS ON A BLACK SHIELD

ZNT-25W
86MM STERLING WITH RED
LETTERS ON A BLACK SHIELD

ZANTOP INTERNATIONAL AIRLINES - ZAN
19 XX - 1995
AIR CARGO CARRIER

• OUT OF BUSINESS IN 1995

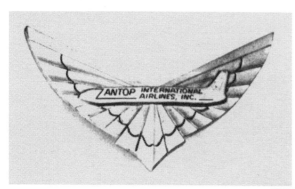

ZAN-10B
SATIN SILVERTONE

ZAN-12W
74MM SATIN SILVERTONE

Appendix 1

A

AAA	AAA AIRLINES
AAH	ALOHA AIRLINES
AAL	AMERICAN AIRLINES
AAM	AIR AMERICA
AAT	AIR ATLANTA
AAX	AAXICO AIRLINES
ABC	ABC AIRLINES
ABX	AIRBORNE EXPRESS
ACD	ACADEMY AIRLINES
ACL	AIR CALIFORNIA - AIR CAL
ACO	AMERICAN CAN CO.
ACU	AIR CARGO, INC.
ACQ	AIR CHAPPARAL
AEC	AERO COMMUTER
AEM	AERO AMERICA
AER	AERO MARINE AIRLINES
AFA	AIR FLIGHT AIRLINES
AFC	AMERICAN FLYERS AIRLINE CORP.
AFL	AIR FLORIDA
AFR	ALFRED FRANK AIRWAYS
AGC	AIR GRAND CANYON
AHO	AIR HOLIDAY
AHW	AIR HAWAII
AIA	ALASKA INTERNATIONAL AIRLINE
AII	AMERICAN INTER ISLAND
AIL	AIR ILLINOIS
AIS	ALOHA ISLAND AIR
AJT	AMERIJET INTERNATIONAL AIRLINE
AKA	ALASKAN AIRWAYS
AKY	AIR KENTUCKY AIRLINES
ALA	ALL AMERICAN AIRLINES
ALC	ATLANTIC COASTAL AIRLINES
ALE	ALLEGHENY AIRLINES
ALG	AIR LOGISTICS
ALH	ALPHA AIR
ALI	ALLIED CHEMICAL CO.
ALL	ALL STAR AIRLINES
ALO	ALLEGHENY COMMUTER
ALS	ALLIED SIGNAL CORP.
ALT	ALTAIR AIRLINES
AMA	AMERICAN AIRWAYS
AMC	AIR MICRONESIA
AME	AMERICAN EAGLE
AMF	AMERIFLIGHT, INC.
AMH	AEROMECH
AMI	AIR AMERICA
AMN	AMERICAN INTERNAT. AIRWAYS
AMR	AIR AMERICA
AMT	AMERICAN TRANS AIR
AMW	AIR MIDWEST
AMY	AMERICAN INTERNAT. AIRLINES
ANE	AIR NEW ENGLAND
ANF	AIR NEW ORLEANS
ANL	AIR NATIONAL
ANV	AIR NEVADA
ANR	AIR NORTH
ANY	AIR NIAGRA
AOA	AIR ONE
AOP	AOPA
AOV	AMERICAN OVERSEAS AIRLINES
APA	APACHE AIRLINES
APC	AIR PAC
APW	ARROW AIRLINES
APX	ASPEN AIRWAYS
AQL	AIRLIFT INTERNATIONAL AIRLINES
AQR	AIR LA
ARC	ARCO OIL CO.
ARE	AIR RESORTS AIRLINES
ARM	ARAMCO
ARZ	ARIZONA AIRWAYS
ASA	ALASKA AIRLINES
ASC	ALASKA COASTAL AIRLINES
ASE	ATLANTIC SOUTHEAST AIRLINES
ASQ	AIR SPUR
ASR	ALASKA STAR AIRLINES
AST	AEROSTAR AIRLINES
ASO	ALASKA SOUTHERN AIRWAYS
ATC	AIR TRANSPORT COMMAND
ATL	ATLANTIC AIRWAYS
ATO	AMERICAN TRANS OCEANIC
AVB	AIR VIRGINIA (AV AIR)
AVM	AIR VERMONT
AWE	AMERICA WEST AIRLINES
AWI	AIR WISCONSIN
AWS	AIR WEST
AXP	AMERICAN EXPORT AIRLINES

B

BAR	BAR HARBOR AIRLINES
BAX	BURLINGTON AIR EXPRESS
BNA	BUFFALO AIRWAYS
BNZ	BONANZA AIRLINES
BOE	BOEING AIRCRAFT CO.
BOI	BOEING AIR TRANSPORT
BOS	BOSTON-MAINE AIRWAYS
BOW	BOWEN AIRLINES
BRA	BRANIFF AIRLINES
BRE	BRANIFF AIR LINES
BRF	BRANIFF INTERNATIONAL AIRLINE
BRN	BRANIFF AIRWAYS
BRT	BROCKWAY AIR (VT)
BRY	BROCKWAY AIR (NY)

BSY	BIG SKY AIRLINES		CTS	CONTINENTAL AIR SERVICE
BTA	BRITT AIR		CTT	CATALINA AIR TRANSPORT
BUR	BURDETT AIR LINES		CXP	CONTINENTAL EXPRESS

C

D

CAA	CIVIL AERONAUTICS ADMIN.		DAL	DELTA AIRLINES
CAB	CABLE AIRLINES		DHL	DHL AIRWAYS
CAC	CONQUEST AIRLINES		DIA	DIAMOND MATCH CORP.
CAL	CARNIVAL AIRLINES		DOL	DOLPHIN AIRLINES
CAM	CATALINA AMPHIBIOUS TRANSP.			
CAP	CAPITAL AIRLINES			

E

CAS	CHRISTMAN AIR SYSTEM		EAA	EXPERIMENTAL AIRCRAFT ASSOC.
CAT	CATALINA AIRLINES		EAL	EASTERN AIR LINES
CBZ	COMBS AIRWAYS		EAT	EASTERN AIR TRANSPORT
CBU	COLORADO AIRWAYS		EIA	EVERGREEN INTERNATIONAL AIRLINE
CCA	CC AIR		ELL	ELLIS AIR LINES
CEN	CENTURY AIR LINES		EMB	EMBRY-RIDDLE
CHK	CHALK'S FLYING SERVICE		EMI	EMPIRE AIR LINES
CHL	CHALLENGER AIRLINES		EMP	EMPIRE AIR LINES
CHP	NORTHERN AIRWAYS		ERA	ERA AVIATION
CHQ	CHAUTAUQUA AIRLINES		EWW	EMERY WORLDWIDE
CKS	KALITTA INTERN. AIRWAYS		EXK	EXECUTIVE AIR
CKW	CARNIVAL AIRLINES		EXP	EASTERN EXPRESS
CLC	CALIFORNIA CENTRAL AIRLINE			
CLE	CALIFORNIA EASTERN AVIATION			

F

CLT	COLONIAL AIR TRANSPORT		FAL	FRONTIER AIRLINES
CLU	COLUMBIA AIRLINES		FDX	FEDERAL EXPRESS
CMM	COMMAND AIRWAYS		FGA	FLORIDAGULF AIR
CMU	COMMUTER AIRLINES		FLA	FLORIDA AIRWAYS
CNP	CENTURY PACIFIC LINES LTD.		FLG	FLAGSHIP AIRLINES
CNT	CENTRAL AIRLINES		FLM	FLEMING INTERNATIONAL AIRLINE
COA	CONTINENTAL AIRLINES		FRE	FREEDOM AIRLINES
COD	CAPE COD AIRWAY			
COL	COLONIAL AIRLINES		FRL	FRONTIER AIRLINE
COM	COMAIR		FSA	FIVE STAR AIRLINES
CON	CONOCO		FTL	FLYING TIGER AIRLINES
COR	CORDOVA AIRLINES			
CPA	CAPITOL AIRLINE			

G

CPI	CAPITOL INTERNATIONAL AIRLINE		GAA	GREAT AMERICAN AIRLINES, INC.
CPL	CHAPPARAL AIRLINES		GAR	GARRETT AIR RESEARCH
CPO	CAPITOL AIRLINES		GDY	GOODYEAR TIRE & RUBBER CO.
CRA	CIRCLE RAINBOW AIR		GEE	GENERAL ELECTRIC CO.
CRB	CARIBAIR		GEN	GENERAL AIR LINES
CRO	CROWN AIRWAYS		GIA	GLOBAL INTERNATIONAL AIRWAYS
CRT	CONTINENTAL AIR TRANSP.		GLF	GULF COAST AIRLINE
CSD	CASCADE AIRWAYS		GLK	GREAT LAKES AVIATION
CSO	CHICAGO & SOUTHERN AIRLINE			
CSX	CASINO EXPRESS AIRLINE		GLW	GULF & WESTERN LINE
CTA	CENTRAL AIRLINES		GNA	GREAT NORTHERN AIRLINES
CTI	CONTINENTAL AIRLINES		GPA	GOLDEN PACIFIC AIRLINES
CTL	CATALINA AIR LINES		GUL	GULF AIR LINES
CTR	CATALINA AIRLINES			

GWA	GOLDEN WEST AIRLINES	MAY	MAYFLOWER AIRLINE
GYC	GRAND CANYON AIRLINES	MCL	McCLAIN AIRLINES
		MCU	McCULLOCH AIRLINES
		MDL	MIDLAND AIR EXPRESS
		MDW	MIDWAY AIRLINES

H

HAL	HAWAIIAN AIRLINES
HAN	HANFORD AIR LINES
HAW	HUGHES AIR WEST
HNA	HENSON AIRLINES

I

IMP	IMPERIAL AIRLINES
INC	INTERCONTINENTAL AIRLINES
INI	INTER-ISLAND AIRWAYS
INL	INLAND AIR LINES
INM	INTERMOUNTAIN AIRWAYS
INS	INTERSTATE AIRLINES
IST	INTERSTATE AIRLINES

J

JAM	JET AMERICA AIRLINES
JCS	JET 24 INTERNATIONAL AIRLINE
JED	JET EAST INTERNATIONAL
JEX	JET EXPRESS
JFS	JOHNSON FLYING SERVICE
JIA	JETSTREAM INTERNAT. AIRLINE
JOL	JOLLY VOYAGER AIRWAYS
JON	JOHNSON INTERNATIONAL A.L

K

KEY	KEY AIRLINES
KIA	KIWI INTERNATIONAL AIRLINES
KOD	KODIAK AIRWAYS
KOL	KOHLER AVIATION CORPORATION
KTO	K-2 AIRLINES
KWA	KODIAK WESTERN ALASKA AIRLINE

L

LAA	LOS ANGELES AIRWAYS
LAB	L.A.B. FLYING SERVICE
LAK	LAKE CENTRAL AIRLINES
LHN	EXPRESS ONE INTERNATIONAL
LOF	RESORT AIR
LON	LONG & HARMON AIRLINES
LUD	LUDDINGTON AIR LINE

M

MAC	MACKEY AIRLINES
MAD	MADDUX AIR LINES
MAM	MAMER AIR TRANSPORT
MAY	MAYFLOWER AIRLINE
MCL	McCLAIN AIRLINES
MCU	McCULLOCH AIRLINES
MDL	MIDLAND AIR EXPRESS
MDW	MIDWAY AIRLINES
MDX	MID-WEST AIRLINES
MER	MERCER AIRLINES
MES	MESABA AIRLINES
MGM	MGM GRAND AIR
MHK	MOHAWK AIRLINES
MID	MID-CONTINENT AIRLINES
MIS	MIDSTATE AIRLINES
MNA	MONARCH AIRLINES
MNE	METRO NORTHEAST
MPA	MID-PACIFIC AIRLINES
MOB	MOBIL OIL CO.
MOD	MODERN AIR TRANSPORT
MOR	MORRIS AIRLINES
MRK	MARK AIR
MRQ	MARQUETTE AIRLINES
MRZ	MARTZ AIR
MSE	MESA AIRLINES
MUS	MUSE AIR
MVA	MISSISSIPPI VALLEY AIRLINE
MWC	MIDWAY CONNECTION
MWX	MIDWEST EXPRESS

N

NAA	NORTH AMERICAN AIRLINES
NAR	AIR CONTINENTAL
NAT	NATIONAL AIRLINES
NAW	NATIONAL AIRWAYS
NCA	NORTH CENTRAL AIRLINES
NCO	NORTHERN CONSOLIDATED AIRLINES
NEA	NORTHEAST AIRLINES
NEI	NORTHEAST INTERNAT. AIRWAYS
NOT	NORTHERN AIR TRANSPORT
NPA	NORTH PACIFIC AIRLINES
NPL	NAPLES AIRLINES
NPW	NATIONAL PARKS AIRWAYS
NRG	ROSS AVIATION
NRT	NORTHERN AIR LINES
NSF	NATIONAL SKYWAYS FREIGHT
NTR	METRO AIRLINES (METRO FLIGHT, INC.
NTT	NATIONAL AIR TRANSPORT
NWA	NORTHWEST (ORIENT) AIRLINE
NWL	NORTHWEST AIRLINK
NWW	NORTHWEST AIRWAYS
NYA	NEW YORK AIRWAYS
NYO	NEW YORK AIR
NYP	NEW YORK, PHIL. & WASH AIRWAYS
NYR	NEW YORK, RIO & BUENOS AIRLINE
NYW	NEW YORK AIRWAYS

O

ONA	OVERSEAS NATIONAL AIRWAYS
ORN	ORION AIR
OXY	OXYDENTAL PETROLEUM
OZA	OZARK AIRLINES

P

PAA	PAN AMERICAN WORLD AIRWAYS
PAC	PAN AMERICAN AFRICA
PAF	PAN AMERICAN FERRIES
PAI	PIEDMONT AIRLINES
PAL	PACIFIC AIR LINES
PAK	PACIFIC ALASKA AIRLINES
PAT	PACIFIC AIR TRANSPORT
PAW	PACIFIC ALASKA AIRWAYS
PAX	PACIFIC EXPRESS
PBA	PROVINCETOWN-BOSTON AIRLINE
PCA	PENNSLYVANIA CENTRAL AIRLINES
PDX	PARADISE ISLAND AIRLINES
PEA	PACIFIC EAST AIR
PEN	PENNINSULA (PEN) AIR
PEX	PEOPLEXPRESS
PGM	PAN AM GMRD
PGR	PAN AMERICAN GRACE AIRWAYS
PIL	PHILLIPS PETROLEUM
PIN	PINEHURST AIRLINES
PIO	PIONEER AIR LINES
PIT	PITCAIRN AVIATION
PLG	PILGRIM AIRLINES
PMA	PACIFIC MARINE AIRWAYS
PNA	PENNSLYVANIA AIR LINES
PNC	PENNSLYVANIA-CENTRAL AIRLINE
PNO	PACIFIC NORTHERN AIRLINES
POC	POCONO AIRLINES
PRA	PRESIDENTIAL AIR
PRE	PRECISION VALLEY AVIATION
PRI	PRIDE AIR
PRN	PRINAIR
PRS	PRESIDENTIAL AIRWAYS
PRT	PORTS OF CALL AIRLINES
PSA	PACIFIC SOUTHWEST AIRLINES
PSE	PACIFIC SEABOARD AIRLINES
PXP	PRESIDENTIAL EXPRESS
PXX	PAN AM EXPRESS

Q

QST	QUEST AIR
QXE	HORIZON AIRLINES

R

RAA	REEVE ALEUTIAN AIRWAYS
RAN	RANSOME AIRLINES
RAP	RAPID AIR TRANSPORT
RAR	ROYAL AMERICAN AIRWAYS
RAY	ROYALE AIR LINES
RBM	ROSENBALM AVIATION
RBN	ROBINSON AIRLINES
RBT	ROBERTSON AIRLINES
RDL	RIDDLE AIRLINES
REA	READING AIRLINES
REN	RENOWN AIRLINES
REP	REPUBLIC AIRLINES
RES	RESORT AIRLINES
RHA	ROYAL HAWAIIAN AIR SERVICE
RIA	RICH INTERNATIONAL AIRWAYS
RIO	RIO AIRWAYS
RLT	RELIANT AIRLINES
RMA	ROCKY MOUNTAIN AIRWAYS
RNO	RENO AIRLINES
RYA	RYAN AVIATION
RYL	RYAN AIRLINES
RYN	PHH AIR (RYAN INTERN. AIRLINE)
RYW	ROYAL WEST AIRLINES

S

SAM	UNITED STATES GOVERNMENT
SAP	SOUTHERN AIR TRANSPORT
SAS	SWIFT AIR SERVICE
SAT	SATURN AIRWAYS
SAW	SOUTHERN AIRWAYS
SBN	SUBURBAN AIRLINES
SBR	SABRE AIRLINES
SCE	SCENIC AIRLINES
SCX	SUN COUNTRY AIRLINES
SEA	SEABORD & WESTERN AIRLINES
SHA	SHAWNEE AIRLINES
SHW	AIR SOUTH
SJC	SAN JUAN AIRLINES
SKB	SKY BUS EXPRESS
SKW	SKYWEST
SLK	SLICK AIRWAYS
SMB	SEDALLIA-MARSHALL-BOONEVILLE
SMO	SEAIR
SNB	SUNBIRD AIRLINES
SNJ	SUN JET AIRLINES
SNW	SUN WEST AIRLINES
SOC	SOCONY OIL CO.
SPA	SIERRA PACIFIC AIRLINES
SPI	SOUTH PACIFIC ISLAND AIRWY
SQH	SUSQUEHANNA AIRLINES
SQV	COASTAL AIRWAYS
STA	SOUTHERN AIR TRANSPORT
STD	STANDARD AIR LINES

STO	STOUT AIR SERVICES
STP	ST. PETERSBURG AIRLINE
STR	STAR AIR LINES
STS	STAR AIR SERVICE
STW	STATEWIDE AIRLINES
SUM	SUMMIT AIRWAYS
SUN	SUN AIRE LINES
SUP	SUPERIOR AIRLINES
SWA	SOUTHWEST AIRLINES
SWF	SWIFT AIRE LINES
SWJ	STATESWEST AIRLINES
SWO	SUNWORLD INTERN. AIRWAYS
SWS	SOUTHWEST AIRLINES
SWW	SOUTHWEST AIRWAYS
SWX	SOUTHWEST AIR FAST EXP.
SYM	SIMMONS AIRLINES
SYW	SKYWAYS

T

TAA	TRANS AMERICAN AIRLINES
TAG	TAG AIRLINES
TCO	TRANSCONTINENTAL AIR TRANSP.
TCN	TRANSCONTINENTAL AIRLINES
TCW	TRANSCONTINENT. & WESTERN AIR
TFA	TRANS FLORIDA AIRLINES
TGA	TRANS GLOBAL AIRLINES
TIA	TRANS INTERNATIONAL AIRLINES
TOC	TRANSOCEAN AIRLINES
TOW	TOWER AIR
TPA	TRANS PACIFIC AIRLINES
TPS	TRUMP EXPRESS
TRA	TRANSAMERICAN AIRLINES
TRC	TRANS CARIBBEAN
TRO	AIR MOLOKAI
TRS	TRANSTAR
TSS	TRANS STATES AIRLINES
TTA	TRANS TEXAS AIRWAYS
TUR	TURNER AIRLINES
TVA	TRANSAMERICA AIRLINES
TWA	TRANS WORLD AIRLINES
TXI	TEXAS INTERNATIONAL AIRLINE
TXT	TEXAS AIR TRANSPORT

U

UAL	UNITED AIRLINES
UAT	UNITED AIRCRAFT & TRANSP.
UCA	COMMUTAIR
UNA	UNIVERSAL AVIATION CORP.
UNI	UNIVERSAL AIRLINES
UPS	UNITED PARCEL SERVICE (U.P.S.)
URL	ULTRAIR
USA	US AIR
USC	U.S. CHECK AIRLINES
USL	US AIRLINES
USM	US AIR MAIL
USO	UNITED STATES OVERSEAS AIRLINE
USS	US AIR SHUTTLE
USX	US AIR EEXPRESS
USW	UNITED STATES AIRWAYS

V

VAI	VAIL AIRWAYS
VAL	VALUJET AIR LINES
VAR	VARNEY AIR LINES
VAT	VARNEY AIR TRANSPORT
VIA	VIKING INTERN. AIRLINES
VIK	VIKING AIRLINES
VSL	VARNEY SPEED LINES

W

WAA	WIEN AIR ALASKA
WAE	WESTERN AIR EXPRESS
WAL	WESTERN AIRLINES
WAK	WESTERN ALASKA AIRWAYS
WAW	WINGS AIRWAYS
WCA	WEST AIR
WCT	WEST COAST AIR TRANSPORT
WIA	WINGS OF ALASKA
WIC	WIEN CONSOLIDATED AIRLINE
WIL	WILMINGTON-CATALINA AIRLINE
WIS	WISCONSIN CENTRAL AIRLINE
WOA	WORLD AIRWAYS
WOM	WINGS WEST AIRLINES
WRT	WRIGHT AIR LINES
WSC	WEST COAST AIRLINES
WYM	WYOMING AIR SERVICE

X

XER	XEROX CORPORATION

Y

YOU	YOUNGSTOWN AIRLINES

Z

ZAN	ZANTOP INTERNATIONAL
ZNT	ZANTOP AIR TRANSPORT
ZNA	ZANTOP AIRLINES

BIBLIOGRAPHY

R.E.G. DAVIES, *AIRLINES OF THE UNITED STATES SINCE 1914*, Washington, D.C. U.S.A. : Smithsonian Institution Press, 1982

Gary DiNUNIO, *AIR LINE PILOT : ALPA CARRIERS THROUGH THE YEARS*, Herndon, VA U.S.A., 1991

Erik DEROGEE, *AIRLINES & AIRPORTS - CODING AND DECODING*, Airnieus Nederland, Netherlands 1992

F.E. BUCHER, *JP AIRLINE-FLEETS INTERNATIONAL 82*, Editions jp, Zurich-Airport, Switzerland, 1982

Ulrich KLEE, *JP AIRLINE-FLEETS INTERNATIONAL 93-94* Editions jp, Bucher and Co., Zurich-Airport, Switzerland, 1993

Paul K. MARTIN, *The AIRLINE HAND BOOK*, Cranston, RI, U.S.A. Aerotravel Research

Gunter G. ENDRES, *WORLD AIRLINE FLEETS, 1978*, Middlesex, TW5 0PA, UK, Airline Publications & Sales Ltd.